Charles Baudelaire

Titles in the series Critical Lives present the work of leading cultural figures of the modern period. Each book explores the life of the artist, writer, philosopher or architect in question and relates it to their major works.

In the same series

Michel Foucault
David Macey

Jean Genet
Stephen Barber

Pablo Picasso
Mary Ann Caws

Franz Kafka
Sander L. Gilman

Guy Debord
Andy Merrifield

Marcel Duchamp
Caroline Cros

Frank Lloyd Wright
Robert McCarter

James Joyce
Andrew Gibson

Jean-Paul Sartre
Andrew Leak

Noam Chomsky
Wolfgang B. Sperlich

Jorge Luis Borges
Jason Wilson

Erik Satie
Mary E. Davis

Walter Benjamin
Esther Leslie

Jean Cocteau
James S. Williams

Georges Bataille
Stuart Kendall

Ludwig Wittgenstein
Edward Kanterian

Octavio Paz
Nick Caistor

Charles Baudelaire

Rosemary Lloyd

REAKTION BOOKS

For Sandy Hamrick

Published by Reaktion Books Ltd
33 Great Sutton Street
London EC1V 0DX, UK

www.reaktionbooks.co.uk

First published 2008

Printed and bound in Great Britain
by Cromwell Press, Trowbridge, Wiltshire

British Library Cataloguing in Publication Data
Lloyd, Rosemary
    Charles Baudelaire. – (Critical lives)
    1. Baudelaire, Charles, 1821–1867
    2. Poets, French – 19th century – Biography
    3. Art critics – France – Biography
    I. Title
    841.7

ISBN–13: 978 1 86189 363 5

Contents

Abbreviations

OC   Charles Baudelaire, *Œuvres complètes*,
ed. Claude Pichois and Jean Ziegler (Paris, 1975–6)

C   Charles Baudelaire, *Correspondance*,
ed. Claude Pichois (Paris, 1972)

MOP   Charles Baudelaire/Thomas De Quincey, *Un Mangeur d'opium*, ed. Michèle Stäuble (Neuchâtel, 1976)

All translations are my own.

1

Childhood and Youth

A small medallion offers the earliest known picture of Charles Baudelaire. He is a *collégien*, poised between childhood and adolescence, at that eternal moment he was to describe some ten years later in a poem he sent to the poet, novelist and critic Sainte-Beuve:

> All beardless then, on that old oaken bench,
> More worn and polished than fetters on a chain,
> Buffed through the endless day by flesh of men,
> We sadly hauled our sorrows, cower'd and bent,
> Beneath that square of sky where we knew solitude,
> Where ten years long the child drinks study's bitter brew.
> (*oc*, I, p. 206)

His gaze is wary, slightly resentful, the mouth unsmiling. In his first full-length article on his American alter ego, Edgar Allan Poe, Baudelaire would make the following claim:

> All those who have reflected on their own lives, who have often looked back to compare their past with their present, all those who have adopted the habit of exploring their own psychology with ease, know what an immense part adolescence plays in an individual's ultimate originality. It is then that objects leave their deep trace on the tender and uncomplicated mind. It is then that colours are vivid and that sounds speak a mysterious

Baudelaire as a schoolboy, 1830, medallion.

language. The character, the originality, and the style of an individual are formed by the apparently commonplace circumstances of early youth. If all those who have occupied the world's stage had noted their first impressions of childhood, what an excellent psychological dictionary we would possess! (*OC*, II, p. 253)

The deep traces his childhood left on Baudelaire's mind are an essential part of his creative genius and his personality, and in the little medallion they can be detected already at work on his image of the world.

We might wonder why there is no earlier portrait, no sketch left by his father, an amateur painter. But by 1819, when François Baudelaire married Caroline Defayis, he had reached that age when the pleasures offered by a young wife were doubtless far greater than those of raising a young child. After all, had he lived to see the first publication of *Les Fleurs du mal*, François Baudelaire would have been 98 years old. When the future poet was born, François Baudelaire already had a sixteen-year-old son by his first wife. Charles's first seven years were spent with a father whose mind had been formed before the 1789 Revolution and a mother who, having married at the age of 26, must have felt she had barely escaped the grim fate the nineteenth century reserved for impecunious spinsters.

Looking back at his childhood when he came to put together some notes for a journalist seeking to write a brief biographical sketch, Baudelaire remembered the house in the rue Hautefeuille in Paris's Latin Quarter, with its medieval network of narrow, cobbled streets and grimy buildings. What the future promoter of the modern world would recall was how old-fashioned it all seemed. 'Old furniture from the period of Louis XVI [1774–93],' he recalled, 'antiques from the Consulate [1799–1804], Pastels. The society of the eighteenth century' (*OC*, I, p. 784). Despite the difference in their ages, however, Baudelaire's father left at least one deep and permanent impression on his child's mind: the love of art. His great poem 'The Voyage,' for instance, opens with the following stanza:

> For the child enamoured of prints and maps
> The universe is as vast as his vast appetite.
> How immense is the world in the glow of the lamps!
> To memory's gaze how it all seems trite! (*oc*, I, p. 129)

Baudelaire himself was a child enamoured of images, which he was later to designate as his 'great, unique, and primitive passion' (*oc*, I, p. 701). As he indicates in a brief description of his life and works, his nature had been marked by a 'permanent taste, since childhood, for all images and all forms of representation in the plastic arts' (*oc*, I, p. 785). His father, to whom, with that embellishment of the truth in which the poet frequently indulged when it provided the requisite degree of shock, he referred as a defrocked priest, had indeed been trained through the church and admitted to the priesthood in 1784. He preferred, however, a career as a teacher. An amateur painter – as an adult, Charles Baudelaire would describe his father's work as execrable but, characteristically, seek to preserve it – and a skilled Latinist, François Baudelaire combined these gifts in his position as a tutor to the two young sons of the Duke de Choiseul-Praslin, creating for them an illustrated Latin word book. Among the many images in this vocabulary is one in which a boy whips a top (just as in 'The Voyage' an angel whips the stars in the cosmos), while behind him are a globe of the earth and two prints, one of them a map of the two hemispheres. This is the immense world of childhood imagination, a plaything for a boy to set spinning, but doomed to shrink in adulthood into repetition and banality:

François Baudelaire, *Latin Vocabulary*, 1790s, pen and ink drawing.

What bitter knowledge comes from every change of place!
Monotonous and small today, the world,
Yesterday, tomorrow, forever, reflects our own face,
An oasis of horror where boredom's sands unfurl. (*oc*, I, p. 133)

François Baudelaire's death when Charles was six years old was followed by a brief period that in the poet's no doubt massaged memory would come to be one of blissful closeness to his mother. Writing to her many years later, on 6 May 1861, in a letter in which, as so often, he clearly hoped to manipulate her emotions to his own financial advantage, he claimed that in his childhood he had gone through a stage when he loved her passionately (*c*, II, p. 153). However manipulative this letter might have been, his poetry suggests that there is indisputably a strong element of truth in the recollections of childhood he offers in it. That intense emotion is echoed in other passages in Baudelaire's writings, most strikingly, perhaps, in a letter of April 1860 to his friend and publisher Auguste Poulet-Malassis, justifying his use, in his adaptation of Thomas De Quincey's *Confessions of an English Opium-Eater*, of the expression 'mundus muliebris' (the world, or more precisely the adornments, of women). This passage is important, too, in telling us how Baudelaire expects to be read, the demands he makes of us to read actively, imaginatively, and intelligently:

> As for the rest of your criticism, I reply by the effort of imagination that the intelligent reader has to make: what is it that the child loves so passionately in his mother, his maid, his older sister? Is it simply the person who nourishes him, combs his hair, washes him and rocks him? It is also the caress and the sensual pleasure she gives him. For the child, this caress is expressed without the knowledge of the woman, through all her graces. So he loves his mother, his sister, his nurse, for the pleasant tickle of satin and fur, for the scent of her breasts and hair, for the tinkling of her jewellery, for the play of her ribbons and so forth, for all that *mundus muliebris* beginning with the blouse and expressing itself even in the furniture on which the woman places the imprint of her sex. (*c*, II, p. 30)

That eroticized image of childhood pleasure is also present in one of the prose poems, where a young boy, who stands out for his 'remarkable liveliness and vitality' (*oc*, I, p. 333), tells his friends about a night in which he had to share a bed with the family's maid:

> Because I couldn't sleep, I amused myself while she slept, by running my hand down her arm, her neck and her shoulders. Her arm and neck are much fatter than those of other women

and the skin there is so soft, so soft, that you'd swear it was writing paper or paper made of silk. I liked it so much that I would have continued for a long time had I not been afraid, afraid of waking her up first but also afraid of I don't know what. Then I plunged my head into her hair which hung down her back as thick as a horse's mane, and it smelled as good, believe me, as the flowers in the garden do now. Try to do the same, when you get a chance, and you'll see. (*oc*, I, p. 333)

That intensity of response to skin and hair marks Baudelaire's child as sharply different from those depicted in the writings of his contemporaries and indicates something, too, about his own childhood nature.

Indeed, among his plans for novels and short stories, Baudelaire, who seems never to have been short of such projects, but who rarely found the time or the energy to develop them into finished works, sketched the following personal characteristics: he acknowledges that, when still very young, he delighted in 'skirts, silks, scents, women's knees' (*oc*, I, p. 594), while elsewhere he notes his own 'precocious taste for women', adding: 'I thought the scent of fur was the scent of women. I remember . . . In a word, I loved my mother for her elegance' (*oc*, I, p. 661). In his adaptation of De Quincey's *Confessions* he would put it even more powerfully: 'the precocious taste for the world of women, the *mundi muliebris*, all that shimmering, glittering, and perfumed apparatus, creates the superior genius'. It forms, indeed 'a delicacy of the skin and a distinction of accent, a kind of androgyny, without which the harshest and most virile genius remains, where artistic perfection is concerned, an incomplete being' (*oc*, I, p. 499).

Other memories of this brief period, which Baudelaire's personal myth painted as idyllic, whatever the reality may have been, can be found in both his verse and his prose poems. The plaster Venus mentioned in the inventory of his home at Neuilly, on the outskirts of Paris, where he and his mother spent the summer of 1827, appears for instance in the beautiful little still life included as the untitled poem number 99 in *Les Fleurs du Mal*:

> I still remember, lying near to the city,
> Our little white house, so small but so calm,
> Its plaster Pomona and its old Aphrodite
> In the tiny grove hid naked legs and bare arms.
> How superbly each evening the sun would stream in,
> Through the pane where its sheaf of rays scattered asunder,
> This huge open eye in the curious sky beaming
> Would gaze on our long silent dinners together,
> Pouring the bounty of its candle-like glow
> On our meagre meal and the cheap drapes in the window.
> (*oc*, I, p. 99)

In addition to the Venus, the inventory made at the time of François Baudelaire's death indicates that the library also contained the 1772 *Encyclopédie*, compiled under the guidance of Denis Diderot and Jean-le-Rond d'Alembert, and writings by Voltaire, François Rabelais and the playwright Prosper Crébillon. Voltaire and Rabelais would both figure in Baudelaire's study of laughter, the first as an example of laughter conveying the individual's sense of superiority, the second as the great French master of the grotesque, directly symbolic but always containing an element of the useful and reasonable (*oc*, II, p. 537). In later life, Baudelaire would certainly assert that as a child he had been 'lucky or unlucky enough to read only fat works for adults' (*oc*, II, p. 42), not the nauseatingly moralistic works that all too often passed for children's literature in the early nineteenth century.

The inventory also mentions an album of drawings by the Italian artist Giovanni Piranesi, one of whose plates Baudelaire would rediscover in De Quincey's *Confessions*, in a hallucinating image of the modern individual:

Creeping along the sides of the walls, you perceived a staircase; and upon it, groping his way upwards, was Piranesi himself: follow the stairs a little further, and you perceive it come to a sudden abrupt termination, without any balustrade, and allowing him who had reached that extremity no step onwards, except into the depths below . . . But raise your eyes, and behold a second flight of stairs still higher: on which again Piranesi is perceived, but this time standing on the very brink of the abyss. Again elevate your eye, and a still more aerial flight of stairs is beheld: and there again is poor Piranesi, busy with his upward labours: and so on, until both the unfinished stairs and Piranesi are lost in the upper gloom of the hall. (*MOP*, p. 189)

Baudelaire does not include this passage in his adaptation of De Quincey and he does not mention Piranesi in his later writings, perhaps feeling the painter was too closely associated with an earlier generation of poets, but the image of the artist endlessly climbing an endless and imperfect staircase seems very close to certain aspects of the universe of *Les Fleurs du mal* with its spleen and its pessimism.

However important his father's library may have been in the formation of Baudelaire's mind, it seems to be the case that it did not back onto Charles's nursery, as he claimed in a poem not included in *Les Fleurs du mal*. However this may be, the poem suggests the close relationship between the child and his reading, metaphorically breaking down the physical barriers between the book and the mind:

'The Voice'
My cradle used to rock against a library wall,
A sombre Babel, where novels, science, tales and all,
Where Latin ash and Grecian dust twined in an imbroglio.
All this, when I stood just as tall as an in-folio.

Two voices spoke. The first, insidious and obdurate, said:
'The earth is like the very sweetest bread.
The gift I have is one of boundless pleasure,
You've but to make the earth your appetite's fair measure.'
The other said: 'Come, o come travelling in the mind,
Beyond what's possible, beyond what scholars find!'
Coming from who knows where, caressing the ear,
A wailing phantom that yet fills us with fear,
This voice sang like the wind on the strand.
I answered: 'Sweet voice! I'm yours to command.'
And thus began my flaw and my fatality.
In the vast distance behind the scenery,
In the darkest point of the deep abyss,
I see strange worlds distinctly in my bliss.
Ecstatic victim of my visionary grace,
Foul serpents bite my shoes as on I pace.
It's since that time I share the prophets' taste
For empty seas and for the sandy waste;
Since then I laugh at funerals and weep at feasts,
And wine most men find gall to me tastes sweet;
Since then I think men lie when truth they utter,
And, gazing at the moon, fall in the gutter.
The Voice consoles me saying: 'Let dreams rule;
The wise man dreams less richly than the fool.' (*oc*, i, p. 170)

Travelling beyond the bounds of earth, choosing the impossibilities
of the imagination rather than the greatest joys that mere reality
can provide, was indeed Baudelaire's choice, but much of what
drives his later writing is something far more powerful, more
corrosive and more original than the consolation the Voice
offers here.

Another memory of those early years is captured in the essay
Baudelaire first published in 1851 under the somewhat ironic title

'The Moral of the Toy'. In this essay he recalls a visit he paid as a child to 'the beautiful and generous' Mme Pancoucke, who had studied flower painting under the great rose artist Pierre-Joseph Redouté and whose husband had acted as witness to the marriage of Charles's step-brother Alphonse. Mme Pancoucke was dressed, to the great delight of that 'precocious dandy', the child Baudelaire, in velvet and furs (*oc*, i, p. 580). Entering her apartment, Charles and his mother were struck by an 'extraordinary and truly fairy-like spectacle':

> You could not see the walls, because they were covered in toys. The ceiling disappeared under a flowering of toys that hung like marvellous stalactites. The floor barely offered a narrow path for your feet to follow. Here there was a mass of toys of every kind from the most expensive to the most modestly priced, from the simplest to the most complex. (*oc*, i, p. 580)

It is vital to remember here that Baudelaire describes the toy as the child's 'first initiation into art, or rather, it is in the toy that the child first perceives the realization of art' (*oc*, i, p. 583). This apparently simple tale offers, therefore, a powerful insight into the ways in which the young Baudelaire became aware of the possibilities of art and their close relationships with the senses. The whole of life in a miniature form, but more highly coloured, cleaner and shining more brightly than in the real world, can, Baudelaire tells us, be found in toys.

> In a toyshop you see gardens, theatres, beautiful clothes, eyes as pure as diamonds, cheeks lit by rouge, charming lace, carriages, stables, stalls, drunkards, charlatans, bankers, actors, puppets resembling fireworks, kitchens and entire armies, well disciplined, with cavalry and artillery. (*oc*, i, p. 582)

Toy drunkards? While this sounds more like the Baudelaire of adulthood, it remains the case that the marionette Guignol, beloved of nineteenth-century children, was usually accompanied by a cat, a female companion, Madelon, and a kindly drunkard, Gnafron. First developed in Lyon around 1800, Guignol would have been part of Baudelaire's childhood.

More fascinating still, this collection of toys, unlike the collections of so many adults, had been assembled not to keep, but to give away. 'When a good little boy comes to see me,' Mme Pancoucke explains, 'I bring him here so that he can take away a souvenir of me.' The child immediately reveals how well he has understood this idea. Realizing, instinctively if not rationally, that the richer the gift he requests, the better he will honour her memory, he asks for the 'most beautiful, bright, and bizarre of all the toys' (oc, i, p. 582). For Baudelaire, after all, beauty was always bizarre. Of course his mother, either embarrassed by what she perceived as the child's greed, or determined not to be outdone in her child's memory by this rival, insisted that he select instead 'an infinitely mediocre object' (oc, i, p. 582), which would in turn merely conjure up an infinitely mediocre gift-giver. 'My mother is fantastic,' wrote the adult Baudelaire: 'you have to fear and please her' (oc, i, p. 662). But memory works in such a way that even if the child was forced to accept a less beautiful present, the recollection of that 'Toy Fairy', as he calls her, retains all the power and beauty of the toy initially chosen, since after all what counts is not the object chosen but the act of choosing.

When he came to seek an image of an earthly paradise in the poem 'Moesta et errabunda', he seems to have found inspiration in his memories of this period of his existence, spent with that mother whom he had to fear and please.

But the green paradise of our childish passions,
The races, the songs, the kisses, the flowers,

General Jacques Aupick,
c. 1852, lithograph by
Leon Noll.

The violins throbbing beyond the green mountains,
With the carafes of wine at evening in the bowers,
– But the green paradise of our childish passions,

The innocent paradise of secretive pleasures
Is it already more distant than India or China? (*oc*, I, p. 64)

India: by Baudelairean definition, as we shall see, the land you
never reach. China: the land where you tell the time by gazing into
the eyes of cats (*oc*, I, p. 299).

When Caroline Baudelaire remarried some eighteen months
after François Baudelaire's death, she brought into this close
relationship with her son a man whose ideals were to prove very
different from those of the poet. Jacques Aupick was a soldier,
with the outlook and convictions of a practical man whose career
reflected the rise of the pragmatic, often philistine, middle class
who, after the revolution of 1848, would accept that most bourgeois

of emperors, Napoleon III, in preference to a republic. While the letters Baudelaire wrote as a boy reveal no open hostility towards this new presence in his life, the adult poet's personal mythology painted him in a far darker light. The childhood and youth of the poet Pierre Dupont, Baudelaire would write, in a notice that appeared in 1851 as a preface to the worker-poet's four-volume collection *Chants et Chansons*, 'resemble the childhood and youth of all those destined to become famous. It is very simple and explains the following age. The fresh sensations of family life, love, constraint, the spirit of revolt, all mingle together in sufficient quantity to create a poet' (*oc*, II, pp. 28–9). And he added, in a sentence that has an even more personal tone:

> It is good for every one of us, once in our life, to have experienced the pressure of a hateful tyranny: it teaches us to hate it! How many philosophers have sprung from the seminary! How many rebellious natures have come into being in the shadow of a cruel and punctilious Empire soldier! Oh fertile discipline, how many songs of freedom we owe you! One fine morning the poor, generous nature explodes, the satanic charm is broken, and there remains of it only what is essential, a memory of pain, as yeast to the dough. (*oc*, II, p. 29)

A cruel and punctilious soldier Aupick was probably not, but his arrival in Charles's life coincided with two unhappy events: the beginning of what De Quincey terms 'the horrid world of school', and the family's removal from Paris to Lyon. In the biographical notes Baudelaire jotted down in 1852 in response to a request from the journalist Antonio Watripon, Aupick is not mentioned by name, but we do find the following ominous line: 'After 1830, the Collège de Lyon. Blows, battles, with teachers and classmates. Heavy melancholies' (*oc*, I, p. 784). These brief notes acquire a particular resonance when set in the context of Baudelaire's convictions about the role of childhood in the formation of the adult artist.

In adapting De Quincey's *Confessions of an English Opium-Eater*, Baudelaire devotes a chapter to what he calls 'The Child Genius'. Here he insists that 'all biographers have understood, more or less completely, the importance of anecdotes linked to the childhood of a writer or artist', but he adds:

> I find, however, that this importance has never been affirmed sufficiently. Often, in contemplating works of art, not in their easily-grasped *materiality* . . . but in the spirit with which they are endowed, in the atmospheric impression they contain, in the spiritual light or darkness they shed on our souls, I have felt myself visited by a kind of vision of their authors' childhood. Certain little disappointments, certain little joys of childhood, swollen out of all proportion by an exquisite sensitivity, become later on in the adult's life, even unbeknownst to that adult, the seed of a work of art. (*oc*, i, pp. 497–8)

That beautifully and powerfully expressed link between the artist's childhood and adult creativity, especially the 'spiritual light or darkness' a work conveys, is vital to our understanding of Baudelaire's own works. The seed of many of Baudelaire's verse and prose poems can be found in his own childhood, however much the initial cause may have 'swollen out of all proportion'.

The memories school left him can be gauged from a paragraph commenting on Poe's story 'William Wilson', and particularly the passage concerning the protagonist's school days:

> What do you say about that bit? Don't you think that the char- acter of this singular man is already somewhat clearer? As for me, I can feel rising up from this description of school a black perfume. I feel circulating in it the shudder of dark years of

being kept under lock and key. The hours passed in the lockup, the unease of a frail and abandoned child, the terror caused by the master, our enemy, the hatred of tyrannical classmates, the solitude of the heart, all these tortures of youth, Edgar Poe did not experience them. (*oc*, II, p. 257)

Poe might not have done so, but the sentence structure invites us to believe that Baudelaire did, and the biographical notes he later wrote intensify that image by their references to his unhappiness at his school in Lyon. The solitude attributed to William Wilson as a schoolboy, the solitude emphasized in the poem sent to Sainte-Beuve, finds a further parallel in *My Heart Laid Bare*, as Baudelaire called the notes jotted down with the aim of writing his confessions: 'a sense of *solitude*, ever since childhood. Despite the family – and especially in the midst of my classmates – a feeling of an eternally lonely destiny' (*oc*, I, p. 680). And yet, he adds, significantly, 'a very keen taste for life and for pleasure'. We find an analogous contradiction a little later in *My Heart Laid Bare*: 'Even as a young child I felt two contradictory sentiments in my heart, the horror of life and the ecstasy of life.' And he refines this complex depiction by adding a caustic self-judgement: 'Absolutely typical of an excitable layabout' (*oc*, I, p. 703).

His time at school in Lyon also felt like an exile because he was remote from the city in which he had been born and which was most familiar to him. As early as July 1832, when he had been in Lyon for only half a year, Baudelaire was writing to his half-brother Alphonse that he detested the people of Lyon, whom he found dirty, greedy and self-centred, the terms being almost identical with those with which, at the end of his life, he would castigate the Belgians. 'I am horribly unhappy with the school, which is dirty, badly run, disorderly, and where the students are nasty and dirty like all those from Lyon' (*c*, I, p. 80). He was not alone in that view of the school, which other pupils also described as filthy and poorly run. By September, however, things had improved, at least on the home front. The family lodgings were charming and commanded a magnificent view over a hill whose rich green colour inspired the future art critic's fervent admiration. By November 1833 changes taking place in the city were attracting his interest, and inspiring a passage revealing the pleasure he took in flexing his writing muscles:

In Lyon they are building a *suspension bridge* over the River Saône, entirely in iron. All the shops are going to be lit by gas; they are digging up all the streets. The Rhône, that rapid river with its sudden floods, is going to overflow again. For it's raining a great deal just now in Lyon. The glass factory situated on a peninsula close to the city (for we college boys went there on an outing), well, the Rhône is constantly eating away at the isthmus, it gnaws and chews. Last night it finally carried the isthmus away. These are things that often happen in the Rhône. An irregularity becomes an inlet, a spit of land becomes an island; for the river is very fast flowing. (*c*, I, p. 20)

In letters like this the future poet of modernity appears in embryo, both in his subject matter and in the palpable delight in finding the correct term – isthmus, peninsula, irregularity.

Nevertheless, his displeasure with Lyon lingered. In a letter to his half-brother dated New Year's day 1834 he wrote about his jubilation at the thought of returning to the capital. 'I miss the boulevards, Berthellemot's sweets and Giroux's general store, and the rich bazaars where you find everything you need to make fine gifts. In Lyon there is only one shop for fine books, two for cakes and sweets and so on' (*c*, I, p. 23). Fine books: all his life, even in extreme poverty, Baudelaire would seek out fine books, having those he bought or received as gifts beautifully bound, as though their precious contents gained further value through being placed in a correspondingly beautiful container. Already in a letter to Alphonse dated 23 November 1833 he thanks his half-brother for a gift of a 'fine edition of Juvenal'. And the boulevards: barely into his teens Baudelaire already has the mentality of the *flâneur*.

For decades after he had left it, Lyon, like Brussels at the end of the poet's life, would continue to arouse his scorn and ire. It is as if, however much he might rage against Paris from time to time, he needed to have a personal atlas of cities that were even worse. Thus we find him, in 1845, when he came to write his account of the annual art exhibition known as the Salon, summarily (and unjustifiably) dismissing Lyon as 'painting's penal colony' (*oc*, ii, p. 395). In the 'Salon of 1846', Lyon is depicted as 'that city of shop-counters, a bigoted and fussy city, where everything, even religion itself, has to have the calligraphic clarity of a cash register' (*oc*, ii, p. 462). An unfinished article on philosophical art continues to castigate Lyon as a strange, narrow-minded city of shopkeepers, 'full of fog and coal', 'misty and sooty', a place where ideas are tangled and brains blocked up like a stuffy nose (*oc*, ii, p. 601). As Byron, a poet Baudelaire much admired, has observed: 'hatred is by far the longest pleasure; / Men love in haste, but they detest at leisure' (*Don Juan*, canto xii, stanza 6). Baudelaire himself would write, in one of his earliest published essays: 'hatred is a precious liquor, a poison more costly than that of the Borgias – for it is made with our blood, our health, our sleep and the best part of our love! We must be chary of using it!' (*oc*, ii, p. 16). Good advice, no doubt, but, as is the fate of most good advice, destined to be ignored.

By the beginning of 1836 the Aupicks returned to Paris and Baudelaire was sent to school at the Lycée Louis-le-Grand. The curriculum he followed both in Lyon and in Paris was largely classical, allowing him to develop that fine knowledge of Latin that underpins much of his sensitivity to the French language. De Quincey's *Confessions* contain an illuminating commentary that Baudelaire included in his adaptation of the work:

at fifteen my command of [Greek] was so great that I not only composed Greek verses in lyric metres, but could converse in Greek fluently, and without embarrassment – an accomplishment . . . which, in my case, was owing to the practice of daily reading off the newspapers into the best Greek I could furnish *extempore*: for the necessity of ransacking my memory and invention, for all sorts and combinations of things, &c., gave me a compass of diction which would never have been called out by a dull translation of moral essays. (*MOP*, p. 109)

In translating this passage, Baudelaire transforms 'compass of diction' into 'un dictionnaire toujours prêt', an ever-ready dictionary, a term that is central to his aesthetics. While Baudelaire was not quite so dedicated a classicist, he too came to find for the modern world a complexity of vocabulary that stems in large measure from his classical training. At school he also learned some English (most of his knowledge of that language, however, came from his mother, who was born in London and had spent her childhood in England) and some natural history. His studies in this last did not prevent him later from describing a bat banging into walls and bashing its head on rotten ceilings ('Spleen: When the low and heavy sky'), but they did include some lessons in anatomy, enough perhaps to arouse that interest in old anatomy books that eventually inspired his poem 'The Hard-working Skeleton'.

But the 'dark years under lock and key' that Baudelaire refers to in his article on Poe came to an abrupt end in April 1838 when Charles was caught with a note from another pupil. Ordered to hand it over, he chose instead to swallow it. When warned that by this action he exposed his classmate to 'unfortunate suspicions', Charles broke out into what the headmaster in his letter to the Aupicks described as 'sniggers too impertinent to be tolerated'.[1] These sniggers – *ricanements* – have been interpreted in many different ways: embarrassment at the exaggerated importance being placed on his behaviour, a sudden insight into an evil not previously suspected, the explosion of the 'generous nature' Baudelaire mentions as an essential part of the formation, not just of Pierre Dupont, but of any great mind. The essay on laughter that Baudelaire published in 1855, but which seems to have been preoccupying him from at least as early as 1845, when his study of caricaturists was prematurely announced on the back of his review of the artistic Salon of that year, suggests the complexity of laughter and its links with human decadence. 'It is certain', he announces, although he adds the caveat that such certainty depends on considering the question from the orthodox point of view, that 'human laughter is intimately linked to the accident of an ancient fall, of physical or moral degradation' (*oc*, ii, pp. 527-8). The comic, he affirms later in the essay, 'is one of humanity's most obvious satanic signs and one of the numerous pips contained in the symbolic apple' (*oc*, ii, p. 530). Laughter becomes in this vision a symptom of the individual's belief in his own superiority, but it is also a mark of weakness: 'indeed,' he asks caustically, 'what more obvious sign of debility could there be than a nervous convulsion, an involuntary spasm like a sneeze?' (*oc*, ii, p. 530). That involuntary spasm, a combination of a conviction of superiority and a sign of weakness, cost the young Baudelaire his place at the Lycée Louis-le-Grand.

Expelled from the Lycée, he was enrolled as an external pupil at the Collège Saint-Louis and, despite numerous problems of discipline and lack of motivation, described by Charles in a letter to his mother as a 'glum and stupid indolence' (*c*, i, p. 75), he passed his Baccalaureate exam on 12 August 1839. 'My exam', he wrote to his step-father, 'was pretty mediocre, except for Latin and Greek – very good – and that is what saved me' (*c*, i, p. 77). Not 'very good' as it happens: the result card clearly shows that even for these subjects he was judged only to be 'good'. Later he would apparently convince his likeable but gullible friend Charles Asselineau that he had been allowed to pass as an act of indulgence to an 'idiot child'.[2] This information Asselineau faithfully passed on to Théophile Gautier, who was preparing an essay on Baudelaire for the forthcoming edition of his works, and Asselineau added: 'He himself told me this.' Reading this naive statement, it is impossible not to see Baudelaire the creator of legends, the builder of a personal mythology, the puller of countless legs, squatting behind Asselineau, convulsed with laughter at his friend's unshakeable credulity.

Summing up his position to his half-brother in August of 1839 the newly qualified Baudelaire wrote:

> So the last year [of school] has ended, and I am going to start another kind of life. It strikes me as strange, and among the many anxieties that seize me, the strongest is the choice of a future profession. It already preoccupies me and torments me, all the more so because I don't feel I have a vocation for any-thing, and I feel I have many different tastes all dominating my thinking one after the other. (c, I, p. 78)

In which, of course, he is not very different from most adolescents, but then, Alphonse and he had never been very close, separated both by that gap of sixteen years and even more by the gulf between their mentalities, and he is unlikely to have been the companion Baudelaire would have chosen to entrust with his deepest secrets, hopes or fears.

Thinking back to this period the adult Baudelaire would recall: 'Travels with my step-father (Pyrenees). Free life in Paris. First literary relationships' (oc, I, p. 784). In fact, the trip to Barèges, in the Pyrenees, where his parents were staying, had taken place a year earlier, in the summer of 1838. The journey back to Paris had led him to travel through what he was to call 'France's most beautiful country', the region around Bagnères in the Pyrenees. Not surprisingly, at a period when many people enjoyed writing poetry,[3] it inspired some verse:

> High above, high above, far from roads that are sure,
> From farmsteads and valleys, beyond the last foothill,
> Beyond all the forests, the carpets of verdure,
> Beyond the last meadows trodden by cattle,
>
> You find a dark lake in a gulf fathoms deep,
> Formed by some desolate peaks white with snows;
> The waters lie tranquil, eternally sleep,
> Never once breaking their stormy repose. (*oc*, I, p. 199)

And so on, until the last stanza:

> And when by sheer chance a wandering cloud
> Darkens in its flight the lake as it lies,
> You'd think it's the cloak or the transparent shroud
> Of a spirit that wanders and moves through the skies. (*oc*, I, 200)

Which, though perfectly competent, is hackneyed enough for anyone to be taken aback if its originator announced he had found his vocation and it was that of a poet. Nevertheless, Baudelaire would take up this poem again much later and rework it for the prose poem 'The Cake' where the emotions of the adolescent observer are now overshadowed by the adult's inescapable irony, youth's happy anticipations shrinking into the mere memory of experience.

> I was travelling. The landscape in which I found myself was of irresistible nobility and grandeur. No doubt something of it passed at that moment into my soul. My thoughts fluttered about, as light as the atmosphere. Vulgar passions, like hatred and profane love, now struck me as being as far away as the

clouds that processed by in the depths of the abysses that lay
beneath my feet. My soul seemed to me as vast and pure as the
cupola of the sky that enveloped me. The memory of earthly
things reached my soul only in feeble and diminished form,
like the sound of bells on imperceptible animals feeding far
off, very far off, on the slope of another mountain. On the little
motionless lake, so immensely deep that it appeared black,
there passed from time to time the shadow of a cloud, like the
reflection of the cloak of a winged giant flying through the sky
. . . I even believe that in my perfect beatitude and utter forget-
fulness of all earthly evil, I had reached the point where I no
longer found so ridiculous those newspapers that claim that
man is born good. (*oc*, I, pp. 297–8)

At which point, predictably, human nature and poetic irony step in:
the narrator, whom hunger has made suddenly aware of his physical existence, takes out a loaf of bread, and is instantly confronted
by two small boys, from whom the bread acquires the appellation
of 'cake' and who all but tear each other's eyes out in an attempt
to get some for themselves. The remembered beauty of a journey
taken in adolescence now forms a sardonic backdrop to the mordant
rejection of any claim of the innate goodness of humanity.

In the autumn of 1839 Baudelaire enrolled in law school, no
doubt on the advice of his half-brother Alphonse, himself a lawyer,
but his energies seem to have been entirely expended in other ven-
ues. It was about this time that he suffered from his first bout of
venereal disease, apparently caught from a cross-eyed prostitute
known as Sara. The cure, which he obtained with the help of his
step-brother, involved the use of opiates, and brought with it not
only stomach cramps and headaches but also an increased sense of
tedium. Thanking Alphonse for his assistance, both practical and
financial, Baudelaire announced an ambitious programme of reading and study, in a pattern of promises that had its roots in his

childhood and would continue throughout his life: 'I am going to plunge into learning, now; I am going to take it up all over again, *law, history, mathematics, literature*. I'll forget in Virgil all the world's pettiness and dirtiness. At least that doesn't cost anything and doesn't make you ache all over' (*c*, i, p. 80). Study as preferable to venereal disease and its cure: however accurate this might be, it is not a particularly promising outlook. Indeed, the study of the law seems to have been rapidly abandoned, although Baudelaire, a voracious reader then and throughout his life, is frequently depicted as lost in a book. The realist artist Gustave Courbet, for instance, shows him so deeply immersed in his reading that he is apparently unaware of his mistress standing behind him. Baudelaire would later request that Jeanne's image be removed from this painting, hence her ghostly presence.

Between leaving school in 1839 and his sea voyage in 1842 Baudelaire would live in the Pension Bailly, on the place de l'Estrapade in the heart of Paris's Latin Quarter. Near to the monumental Panthéon, where the nation buried its famous dead (Mirabeau, Voltaire and Rousseau already reposed there, and in 1885 Victor Hugo's ashes would join theirs), close to the Sorbonne, as well as the Law School, it was also conveniently near the Luxembourg Gardens and the cabarets, theatres, restaurants and pleasure domes of the rue de la Gaîté. Looking back at this blissful period of their lives much later on, when Eugène Crépet asked them for their memories of the youthful Baudelaire in view of the biography he was preparing, several of the friends he had made at this time produced remarkable pen portraits. Gustave Le Vavasseur, of whom Baudelaire was to leave a memorable image in which the minor poet's love of acrobatic exercises is perfectly paralleled by his delight in difficult poetic forms (*oc*, ii, pp. 179–81), sets up a kind of double silhouette:

Gustave Courbet, Charles
Baudelaire reading: detail
from *L'Atelier du Peintre*,
1854–5, oil on canvas.

Baudelaire wrote poetry and so did I. We were bound together
by tender friendship . . . It was meant to be, given that we had
very different characters, highly dissimilar bearing and the most
diametrically opposed outward appearance. He was dark and I
was blond; he was of average height and I was very short; he
was as thin as an ascetic and I as plump as a monk; he was both
distinctive and distinguished while I was simultaneously original
and common; he kept himself as clean as an ermine and I was
as shaggy as a mongrel; he used to dress like a secretary at the
British embassy and I like a ticket-seller; he was reserved and I
outspoken; curiosity drove him to libertinage whereas indolence
drove me to morality; he was a Pagan out of a sense of revolt and
I a Christian out of obedience; he was caustic and I was indul-
gent; he used to torment his mind to mock his heart while I let
the two of them trot along together in tandem etc. etc.[4]

The art lover Jules Buisson, who clearly did not share Baudelaire's belief in the importance of androgyny for the artist, described him as having a 'very delicate nature, very refined, original and tender but feminine and weak', adding, in a judgement that Jean-Paul Sartre would later seize on, that Baudelaire's 'weak and feminine' nature had shattered at its first collision with life.[5] Buisson adds: 'There was one event in his life that he could not bear: his mother's second marriage. On that subject he was unstoppable and his wound still bled.'[6] It is interesting to speculate on the point at which Baudelaire made this event such an important part of the legend he promoted about himself. It is also arresting that it was primarily a critique of his mother: Buisson does not attach it to any hatred of Aupick at this stage. Indeed, however much his step-father may have enraged him, it was really only his mother who counted in his life. The father-figure is, for example, completely elided from the poem 'Benediction' which describes the childhood of a poet.

It is from this period that Baudelaire's love of pantomime and his admiration for the mime Jean-Gaspard Deburau date; he was to call Debarau in 1846 the 'true contemporary Pierrot, the Pierrot of modern history' (*oc*, II, p. 451). Popular theatre, with its potent symbolism, its heightened gestures and its powerful simplification of human problems, finds its way into several of his verse and prose poems. Among these one could quote, for example, the 49th poem of *Les Fleurs du mal*, 'The Irreparable', with its last two stanzas:

– I have seen at times on a commonplace stage
Enflamed by a booming band,
A fairy light up a miraculous dawn
On a sky marked with hell's own brand,
I have seen at times on a commonplace stage

A being, made of gold, light and gauze,
Hurl the enormous Satan down;

But my heart, where ecstasy never calls
Is a stage where you wait in vain
For the being with wings of gauze. (*oc*, i, p. 55)

This fascination with the popular theatre is also reflected in Baudelaire's novella *La Fanfarlo* and in several passages of his art criticism, and it may well find a further indirect reflection in the paintings and etchings of Edouard Manet, the artist who was one of Baudelaire's closest friends in the last years of his life.

It seems that it was in these early years of liberty in Paris that Baudelaire realized, as he was to put it much later in a projected but never completed preface for *Les Fleurs du mal*, that, since 'illustrious poets had already long ago divided up amongst themselves the most flower-strewn provinces of the poetic park' (*oc*, I, p. 181), he himself needed to turn away from those over-worked fields and seek something new. Poems like the one inspired by his trip to the Pyrenees would never make his name in a city teeming with minor versifiers and dominated by the major voices of Victor Hugo, Théophile Gautier, Alphonse de Lamartine and Alfred de Musset. A poem dating from this time, 'No Society Lady' ('Je n'ai pas pour maîtresse'), makes clear what it meant for him to be a writer.

> No society lady is my little tart,
> The Tramp of my soul borrows all of her finery.
> Her beauty flowers only in my cheerless heart –
> Hidden from the gaze of the world and its ribaldry.
>
> For a pair of high heels she sold off her soul;
> But the good Lord would laugh if, simply to spite her,
> I aped old Tartuffe and looked down on my doll,
> Since I sell my thoughts and proclaim I'm a writer.
> (*oc*, I, p. 203)

And the young would-be writer goes on to give a parody of those love poems in which the beloved's charms are dotingly listed. No sparkling eyes here, for the woman in question squints; her breasts, unlike those of most her poetic counterparts, droop down like gourds. But the poet rebukes those who despise this 'impure pauper' forced by hunger to sell her body:

> For that little gypsy's my queen and my regent,
> My pearl, my gem, she is all of my art,
> She who has rocked me on her lap triumphant,
> And between her two hands has warmed up my heart.
> (*oc*, I, p. 203)

Well might he proclaim in a dry little two-liner: 'Here lies one, who having too well loved the whores, / Went down still young to where the blind mole bores' (*oc*, i, p. 205).

Baudelaire would not include 'No Society Lady' in *Les Fleurs du mal*, but there are echoes of it, together with the bizarre adornments of his squinting mistress, in the poem 'Macabre Dance'. More importantly, sympathy for the poor and refusal to sugar-coat his image of them would stay with him, making him markedly different, in his bleak realism and his refusal to present himself as better than the city's outcasts, from the majority of those writing at that time. One final point arises from this poem: what the squint-eyed mistress most fears in 'the cruel night' is seeing the ghosts of her dead lovers. Dead from what cause? The obvious and grim answer is syphilis, one of the great scourges of the age and all the greater for being euphemistically swept under the carpet as a 'maladie honteuse', a shameful disease. It would haunt Baudelaire, too, for the rest of his brief life.

It is possible that a version of this poem dates from as early as 1841. But at that stage Baudelaire was still waiting for something that would provide the great surge of energy that would transform him into a true poet, whereas at this stage he was merely a competent rhymester, one who drew inspiration from that art of counter-idealization of the beloved that marks a wealth of baroque poets but is not in itself a sign of either genius or individuality. The 'explosion' that he singles out as central to the formation of Pierre Dupont, and that he suggests is vital to all writers of originality, still had not taken place. Later, in presenting the work of Edgar Allan Poe, he chose to open with this striking assertion:

Some destinies are fatal: there exist in the literature of every country men who bear the word *jinx* written in mysterious letters in the sinuous furrows of their brows. Some time ago, there came before the tribunals an unfortunate who had on his brow this bizarre tattoo: *out of luck*. Thus he bore everywhere with him the brand of his life, as a book bears its title, and questioning showed that his life had been consistent with the sign. In literary history, there are similar fortunes. (*oc*, ii, p. 249)

And he names two writers he particularly admired and who shared this fate with Poe: the German writer of the fantastic, E.T.A. Hoffmann, and the French novelist Honoré de Balzac. It seems likely that as early as his late adolescence he was seeking his own misfortune in productive rivalry with theirs. We see echoes of this in Buisson's evocation of him endlessly lamenting his mother's second marriage, as though that could somehow weigh in the scale with the misfortunes of Poe, Hoffmann and Balzac. But the real explosion, the real cause of an outburst of that energy which, as Stendhal famously said in *Le Rouge et le Noir*, leads to sublime achievements, came from a different source. According to Buisson, Baudelaire's complaint concerning this second marriage focused on his mother, but he was too close to her, and would remain too emotionally dependent on her all his life, for her to cause that liberating and enabling burst of energetic hatred. The 'vast and vital energy' he admired in Poe (*oc*, ii, p. 317) needed to be set free by a quite different mechanism, a sudden constraint imposed on what he saw as his 'free life in Paris'.

In 1841 the young Baudelaire had run up so many debts in anticipation of the money he would inherit from his father when he turned twenty-one, that a family trust was set up, largely on the urging of his stepfather Aupick, to arrange for a loan on his behalf and to attempt to impose on him what many of his contemporaries would have been delighted to accept, a sea voyage to India. In his brief biographical notes, and in many of the conversations he is reported to have had with friends, Baudelaire would later claim that he did indeed travel to India. 'Travels in India (by mutual consent):

first adventure, the ship dismasted; (Captain Adam [*sic.* for Saliz]). Mauritius, Reunion, Malabar, Ceylon, Hindustan, the Cape: happy wanderings. Second adventure. (Return on a ship without provisions and sailing low in the water)' (*oc*, I, p. 784). Whether or not he undertook the voyage by 'mutual consent', the facts of his itinerary are rather different. Although, on 9 June 1841, he boarded the *Paquebot des mers du sud* bound for Calcutta, the young black sheep was never to complete that voyage. The Captain's name was Saliz: could it be that writing these notes a decade after the event, Baudelaire's memory or imagination supplied the more metaphorically suggestive name of Adam? After a violent storm, in which the ship was indeed dismasted and needed the assistance of an American vessel, the *Thomas Perkins* (named for Boston's so-called 'King of Shipping'), the *Paquebot des mers du sud* limped into Port Louis on Mauritius Island on 1 September. While it was being repaired, Baudelaire stayed with a Creole gentleman, Adolphe Autard de Bragard, whose wife would inspire the sonnet 'To a Creole Lady'. Just over two weeks later, on 18 September, Baudelaire rejoined the ship and travelled with it to the island of Reunion, at which port he disembarked, flatly refusing to go any further. He stayed on Reunion until 4 November, when he boarded the *Alcide*, headed back to France.

No letters from Baudelaire to his parents have been found for this period of his life. Reports from other passengers – or anonymous descriptions purporting to be from other passengers – present him as displaying a range of behavioural patterns, from quiet bravery during the storms encountered, to 'eccentric conduct', including establishing a relationship with a beautiful and passionate coloured woman, who pursued him so ardently that she had to be confined to her cabin for the duration of the voyage (Claude Pichois quotes this account, published just after the poet's death, with the scepticism it deserves).[7] But whatever the truth, and whatever the reasons that prompted him to abandon his journey, apart from the deep longing for Paris that he mentions to Autard de Bragard (c, i, p. 89), the voyage left him with a rich array of memories of the sea, a familiarity with exotic vegetation, some useful vocabulary and a series of metaphors based on journeys.

While some of those images of the ocean were enhanced and inflected by later visits to his mother's house in the little sea port of Honfleur, where he could admire the sea, the ships and the marine sunsets without leaving land, and other images of the sea may reflect not personal experience so much as a literary desire to rival Victor Hugo, whom Baudelaire acknowledged as a master of marine poetry, others seem to spring more directly from this voyage. 'Exotic Perfume' for instance, a version of which his friend Prarond recalled hearing as early as 1842, offers a vignette of a lazy island, with strange trees and tasty fruit, women whose eyes astonish the viewer by their frankness (shades of the coloured woman reported to have pursued him, perhaps?), and a port filled with sails and masts, which he describes, using the correct maritime term (*fatigué*), as weary after their sufferings on a long voyage.

Although he announced to his step-father on 16 February 1842 that he had come back with his pockets full of wisdom, there is, even in this brief letter, a smouldering sense of outrage. 'I am returning without a penny *and I often lacked things I needed*', he affirms, adding, ambiguously: 'If I were to write to you everything I thought and imagined far from you, my writing pad would not be big enough; so I'll say it to you' (c, i, p. 90). It was open to his parents to read contrition and resolutions of better behaviour in future in this claim. With the benefit of hindsight we can be considerably more sceptical.

2

Revolt

The ill-starred poet, rejected by his family, despised by the multitude and starving to death in his garret, was a standard element of Romantic mythology well before Paul Verlaine published his *Poètes maudits* in 1884. That Baudelaire was already beginning to work his way into a personal variant of the myth in his early twenties is obvious from reports of his friends from the Pension Bailly, in the days before his aborted voyage to India, when he constantly harped on the misfortune of his mother's rejection of him, as revealed by her remarriage. He was to find stronger claims still. On his return, although he alleged that now he had 'wisdom in his pockets', he seems to have been increasingly driven by a sense of rage and revolt against the values embodied by his mother, step-father and half-brother, an anger that found a useful parallel in the political events of a country growing increasingly unwilling to accept the leadership of Louis-Philippe's bourgeois monarchy.

He missed out on one source of repression: in early March, just after getting back to Paris, he was obliged by law to enter his name in the lottery for military service. His future admiration for the great soldier-poet Alfred de Vigny is not sufficient to suggest he would have taken on the constraints and demands of the army with stoicism or even resignation. Nevertheless, given his step-father's career, and the complex aura that Napoleon's legacy had conferred on the army, it is not surprising that there should be frequent references to the military in his diaries. As a child,

Baudelaire remarks at one point, 'I wanted to be either a pope, but a military pope, or an actor' (*oc*, i, p. 702), while a jotting in his private diaries claims that there are only three respectable beings: the priest, the warrior, the poet, and adds, in one of those highly condensed verbal bombs in which he excelled: 'knowledge, killing, and creation' (*oc*, i, p. 684). Another passage extends this thought: 'There is nothing great among men except the poet, the priest and the soldier. He who sings, he who blesses, he who sacrifices, and is sacrificed. The rest are made for the whip' (*oc*, i, p. 693). In another section of the diaries he collates military metaphors culled from his reading and from conversations, derisively judging that 'all this glorious phraseology is generally applied to pedants and bar flies'. 'This habitual use of military metaphors,' he adds, 'indicates minds that are not militant but rather made for discipline, that's to say, for conformity, minds born domesticated, Belgian minds, that can think only in society' (*oc*, i, p. 691). It is hard to imagine Baudelaire at any point submitting to the kind of discipline he would have encountered in the army. As it happened, the lottery exempted him.

Freed from that incongruous destiny, he informed his family that he wanted to be a writer. No doubt there were protests and outbursts, but it is unlikely that he provoked quite so Gothic a response as he suggests is the poet's lot in his poem 'Benediction':

> When, following a decree of the powers supreme
> The Poet arrives in this dull world of ennui
> His horrified mother is driven to blaspheme
> And revile the Lord, who is filled with pity.
>
> 'Better to have given birth to a nest of serpents,
> Than ever have nourished such a pitiful thing,
> Cursed be the night with its pleasures so transient
> When my womb conceived expiation for my sin'. (*oc*, i, p. 7)

While the evidence we have of Mme Aupick's style suggests that it is highly unlikely that she uttered anything quite so powerful, she did write to the family lawyer, Narcisse Ancelle, expressing her dismay at her son's cynicism around the time when he had declared his determination to become a writer:

> That sovereign scorn for humanity, his rejection of any belief in virtue, saying he believes in nothing, all of that is terrifying and distressing to me. The whole thing worries me and frightens me; for it seems to me that there is only a step between believing in no honest sentiments and committing an evil action, and the mere thought of it makes me shudder. And I was taking comfort in the belief that my son, despite his lack of order and all his wild ideas, was filled with a sense of honour and that I didn't need to fear any vile act on his part.[1]

Someone with a greater share of worldly wisdom would have seen this as a fairly normal desire for independence, and waited for it to pass.

On 9 April 1842 Baudelaire turned twenty-one and some two weeks later he came into the property inherited from his father; the money he had been so eager to spend since he was eighteen that he had begun building up the debts that would plague him for the rest of his life. His inheritance came in the form of nearly two hectares of land on what was then the edge of Paris, shares and other investments amounting to some 15,000 francs, and a further sum of about 18,000 francs in cash. While he was not rich, he was, as Claude Pichois indicates, well off.[2] In the conviction that he was now easily able to do so, he began to spend lavishly, and soon convinced himself that, as he derisively put it later, 'the mind of every shop-keeper is completely vitiated' (OC, I, p. 703). For instead of prudently investing his money, the young man set about joyously squandering it on clothes and paintings and using it to help pay off debts already accumulated. It is as if he were determined to prove Balzac right in depicting Paris as governed by two things only: gold and pleasure.

He rapidly became such a spendthrift that on 11 June 1843 he sold his land at Neuilly to help cover his mounting expenses. Aware, however, that his family could take legal measures to control his spending, he seems to have made a gesture towards calming their fears in the summer of that year by handing control of his fortune over to his mother and the family lawyer, Ancelle. He agreed to receive a monthly allowance in exchange for a promise not to run up any more debts. But two letters written shortly after this agreement indicate both Baudelaire's inability to conform to any such promise and the extent to which money leapt from his pockets and into the wallets of those vitiated shopkeepers. The first, undated but apparently written in late October 1843, is to his mother, warning her not to take control of his fortune away from him by the legal means of a judicial family council, a *conseil judiciaire*:

> Today I'll send someone to let you know what lodgings I've chosen. – I am perfectly willing to accept the conditions you've laid down. You can come tomorrow and inform the landlord about them. Only there must be no more talk of a *conseil judiciaire*. If I were to find that you had gone ahead with it unbeknownst to me, I would take flight immediately and you would never see me again for I'd go and live with Jeanne. – As I don't want to return to M. Leroy's house, I'm sending you a list of everything I've left there and that needs to be brought by someone who can't give my address. (*c*, I, p. 101)

The blend of guile, self-deception and threats is as typical as that indication at the end of the letter that Baudelaire was already like the man mentioned in 'The Voyage', never losing hope, but in his search for rest constantly running like a madman. The pattern is already established: Baudelaire would spend the next twenty years moving from lodging to lodging, often forced to flee at short notice, leaving behind possessions that might or might not be recuperated by someone who was not in a position to give his new address to those seeking to dun him. Promises would be given in tandem with threats, neither of them sustainable. And for the first time there is in this letter the mention of his lover Jeanne, whose presence, more or less close, more or less destructive, would be one of the few constants in the poet's life.

He had met Jeanne Duval, who also went under various other names, in 1842. The photographer Nadar, who had known her through the theatre where she was a minor actress, and the poet Théodore de Banville, who may also have met her before Baudelaire

Baudelaire, *Une Femme pour Asselineau* (Portrait of Jeanne Duval), 1861, pen and ink drawing.

did, both present her as a woman of colour, exuberant and wild, with a cloud of curly dark hair. Nadar was briefly her lover before she battened on to Baudelaire, for whom she was both a profound source of inspiration and an inescapable burden, the angel and demon who haunts much of the early love poetry of *Les Fleurs du Mal*. He has left several sketches of her, drawings that show her abundant curly hair, tightly belted waist and prominent breasts, as well as her slightly contemptuous gaze. Baudelaire's letters to his mother present Jeanne as having little in common with him, certainly not an interest in his poetry, but in reading those letters we need to remember his relationship with the person to whom he was writing. Whatever the truth may be, he regarded Jeanne in later life as a responsibility it behoved him to bear. It is almost the only one he would accept.

The October 1843 letter to his mother, despite its agreement to accept her conditions regarding his finances, is rapidly followed by a note dated 5 November 1843, in which Baudelaire promises to pay M. Arondel 300 francs by the end of February. Antoine Arondel, second-hand dealer, and Louis Cousinet, restaurant owner, whose demands for payment begin to appear early in 1844, would dog Baudelaire for the rest of his life, and after his death would each demand repayment from the estate, Cousinet sending in a bill for 2,523 francs and Arondel for 15,000.[3] A comment jotted down in the diaries sheds a dubious light on Baudelaire's attitude to living on credit: 'whenever a letter from a creditor arrives, write fifty lines on an extra-terrestrial subject and you will be saved' (*oc*, I, p. 656).

There was no such salvation. Far too much temptation arose from the move to lodgings on the Isle Saint-Louis, although it was at that time an unfashionable area of Paris and therefore less costly than other *arrondissements*. Further expenses accrued from the decision to set Jeanne up in her own establishment on the nearby rue de la Femme-sans-tête (named for an inn sign depicting a head-

Baudelaire, *Jeanne Duval*, with notes in the hand of Poulet-Malassis, 1858–60, pen and ink drawing.

less woman, with the implication that when women could not speak, all was well). The child who, from exile in Lyon, longed to be back in Paris with its well-stocked shops, can still be detected in the young man whose apartment his friend Ernest Prarond was to describe for Eugène Crépet:

It was on the ground floor, a single room, very lofty. You entered it after having passed through the main entrance, by a door on the left. Opposite that door, the fireplace. Between the fireplace and the window, a large chest, in which Baudelaire placed his books and hid his money. There must have been hidden closets for his clothes and his linen . . . Opposite the chest, a sofa. A single very high window looking onto the street; curtains of a heavy material, attractively hung. Opposite that window, at the back of the room, a bed. A few armchairs amongst all that. On the walls were painted canvases, generally old.[4]

The paintings, frequently bought from Arondel, too often proved, predictably enough, not to be of the highest calibre, and a disabused Baudelaire would dispose of them disdainfully, at a financial loss, only to fall victim yet again to the same temptation. He was an avid collector at this period of his life, gathering around him paintings, caricatures and books. His contemporaries leave many little vignettes of him reading those books: Courbet's painting of him deep in a large and somewhat dog-eared volume has numerous written equivalents. In his memoirs, the writer and critic Champfleury, who shared Baudelaire's passion for both caricature and popular theatre, and later for Wagner, depicts him entering casinos with books under his arm, books that ranged from Swedenborg's utopian visions to Wronski's algebra, from poets like Ronsard and Mathurin Régnier to Baudelaire's contemporaries.[5]

While the area where he now lived, on the Isle Saint-Louis, was not at that stage much esteemed by middle-class society, it was frequented by artists and writers. Indeed, living in the nearby Hôtel Pimodan, in far more lavishly furnished rooms than Baudelaire, thanks to the generosity of her lover, Alfred Mosselman, was a young singer and model who would play a role in Baudelaire's image of women: Apollonie Sabatier, nicknamed La Présidente, because she presided over weekly dinners that gathered writers like Gautier and Banville, artists like Fernand Boissard, Ernest Meissonier and Auguste Préault, and the sculptor Ernest Christophe, whose statues would later inspire two of Baudelaire's poems. La Présidente would come to hold an important place in Baudelaire's imagination, if not in his life. It was also at the Hôtel Pimodan, in the rooms of the painter Fernand Boisson, that a similar group of bohemian artists gathered to take what was called 'dawamesk', a concoction based on hashish. A witty self-portrait of this time shows Baudelaire

Vincent Vidal, *Apollonie Sabatier, La Présidente,* ?1850s, crayon and watercolour.

prowling through a nocturnal Paris under the influence of hashish, his head a target for comets while his shoe laces seem to have taken on a life of their own. And Baudelaire would remember these tastings later when he came to write his studies of the 'artificial paradises'.

Furthermore, he was soon to move to the Hôtel Pimodan himself, where he had an apartment his friend Charles Asselineau described as 'princely'. When he came to write his biography of Baudelaire, Asselineau evoked it in these terms:

> During this unknown phase of his life, Baudelaire was lodged in princely fashion in a historic house, that famous Hôtel Pimodan . . . He lived under the attic in an apartment costing 350 francs a

Baudelaire, 'Self-portrait under the Influence of Hashish', *c.* 1842–3, pen and watercolour wash.

year, consisting (what a good memory I have!), of two rooms and a closet. I can still see the main room, which was both bed-room and study, its walls and ceiling hung with red and black wallpaper and lit with a single window whose panes, with the sole exception of the top row, were opaque, 'in order to see only the sky', he used to say . . . Between the alcove and the fireplace I can still see the portrait [of Baudelaire] painted by Emile Deroy in 1843 and on the opposite wall above a divan which was always piled with books, a copy (reduced) of [Delacroix's] *The Women of Algiers*, copied by Deroy for Baudelaire and that he used to show off with great pride.[6]

The portrait by his nineteen-year-old friend Deroy, who would die in 1847, shows an elegant young man, dressed in black, with abundant dark hair, a goatee and a moustache. The collegian's withdrawn glance in the medallion is transformed here into a bold stare at the viewer. He sits in a high-backed armchair, one beautiful hand on the armrest in the foreground of the picture, demanding the viewer's attention. He gazes directly and slightly quizzically at the viewer. This is not yet the face that stares back at

Emile Deroy,
Baudelaire, 1843–4,
oil on canvas.

us from the photos of Nadar or Carjat with such intensity and intellectual suffering.

As Asselineau suggests, however, there are close physical parallels between this young man and the male protagonist of *La Fanfarlo*, the novella Baudelaire published in January 1847 and which several of his friends suggest he began working on as early as 1843. Its central character, Samuel Cramer, is described in the following terms:

> Samuel's brow is pure and noble, his eyes glitter like two drops of coffee, his nose is teasing and mocking, his lips impudent and sensual, his chin square and despotic and his hair pretentiously Raphaelesque. He is simultaneously enormously idle, sadly ambitious and an unhappy star, for all his life he has hardly had a single idea that was more than half-baked. (*OC*, I, p. 553)

Indeed, while *La Fanfarlo* is much more than autobiographical, it seems to be in part a derisory projection of what Baudelaire's life could have been; that of a journalist whose youthful romantic ideals are slowly submerged into anonymous, bourgeois semi-respectability as his poetry is set aside for books written for the masses and his mistress works to ensure he becomes a member of the Institute and receives a medal from the government. The Baudelaire of Deroy's portrait could well have followed such a trajectory, but his image of what it meant to be a writer and what was essential to poetry (now that the 'good days of Romanticism', as he terms them in *La Fanfarlo*, were over), was beginning to take shape as something radically different from, and far more powerful than, Samuel Cramer's poetry volume *Orfraies*. Baudelaire would not have been Baudelaire without Romanticism, but Modernism would not be Modernism without the poet, whose thinking was profoundly shaped by the difficult years leading up to 1848. Towards the end of his life he would jot down in notes for a never completed letter to the facile critic Jules Janin a definition that seems to be a long-held conviction. Why, he truculently demands, must the poet be a maker of sweets? Why should he not instead be 'a grinder of poisons', 'a breeder of serpents for miracles and shows, a snake-charmer in love with his reptiles and enjoying simultaneously the icy caresses of their coils and the terrors of the crowd?' (OC, II, p. 238)

It was in 1842 or 1843 that Baudelaire sent his former school friend Auguste Dozon a sonnet, 'The Bad Monk', that reflects the sharp discrepancy he was feeling between his ambitions and his achievements. In the past, he claims in the quatrains to this sonnet, monks would gaze on the paintings in their monastery or on the tombstones of the cemetery, and through their meditations would both glorify Death and escape from the rigours of their physical situation. The tercets, however, show the poet in a quite different light from those holy monks: my soul, he admits, is a tomb in which I, contemptible hermit, have lived for all eternity, and yet nothing embellishes the walls of my hateful cloister. 'When will I learn to transform the living spectacle of my own sad misfortune into work for my hands and pleasure for my eyes?' (OC, I, p. 16). Even in these early days, he knew that his poetry could not merely rework the timeworn themes but must draw from his own experience and his own vices its strength, its beauty and its modernity. And however anxious he might be to prove himself, the relative paucity of variants from one printed version of a poem to the final version reveals that he was remarkably careful not to publish anything before he was convinced it was ready.

At the time he wrote 'The Bad Monk', Baudelaire was still, as he says of Samuel, 'a sickly and fantastic creature, whose poetry shines more in his person than in his works' (OC, I, p. 553), but he was about to be re-forged in the fire of rage that twice in his life would produce a sudden outburst of creativity, the second being in the period following the trial of Les Fleurs du mal. In May 1844 his family, alarmed to discover that he had spent 20,500 francs since coming into his inheritance, set in motion the procedures necessary for the *conseil de famille* which would permanently remove control of his funds from his own hands and place them in those of the lawyer Ancelle. Announcing, somewhat petulantly and without any doubt foolishly, that he would not discuss his personal affairs in front of strangers, Baudelaire refused even to attend the legal hearing, let alone present his own case. His rage at the result is palpable in a letter written to his mother in the course of that summer:

> You tell me that my anger and unhappiness will soon fade. You assume that you're only hurting me as one hurts a child, for its own good. But there's one thing you need to be sure of, something you always seem to be blind to; it is that truly for my misfortune I am not made like other men. – What you consider as something necessary and hurtful demanded by the occasion, is something I cannot, cannot bear. – It's not hard to explain. You can, when we're alone, treat me however you like – but I will repel with fury everything that impinges on my freedom. – Isn't it incredibly cruel to submit me to the judgement of a couple of men who are bored by the whole affair and who do not know me? Between the two of us, who can boast of knowing me and understanding where I want to go or what I want to do, or knowing how patient I can be? (*c*, I, p. 109)

'I am not made like other men.' It seems likely that by the time he wrote this letter Baudelaire had already made the turn away from that clichéd claim of difference, a cry that young men have made down the centuries, to the sardonic ability to force recognition from those who had rejected him, since 'To the Reader', in which he addresses his reader as his 'semblable', his twin, appears to be an early poem dating from these difficult years. The Baudelaire of 1844 may himself not have known where he wanted to go and what he wanted to do, and may not yet have been possessed of that patience which is, as Buffon asserted, the larger part of genius, but the determination to prove himself in his mother's eyes took on an impetus that, combined with his association with a group of young poets, led to a highly productive surge of creativity.

In verses he addressed to their mutual friend Ernest Prarond, Gustave Le Vavasseur leaves us a rhymed impression of those years of Baudelaire's close friendship and sturdy rivalry with other young poets. While such lines confirm Graham Robb's depiction of the popularity of writing verse in those years, they also suggest the vast gulf between Baudelaire and his friends where the nature and purpose of poetry were concerned.

> It was back in those days when, with love that was fervent,
> We all fell in love with the Muse and her servant;
> All four of us began then to haunt her vast mansion,
> You and me, dear friend, with Baudelaire and Dozon.
> How madly we loved to make rhymes; Baudelaire
> Far more than to please sought to make readers stare.
> Was he fearful of seeing in childish apprehension
> His Muse's originality in all of its tension?
> And his unfettered mind, was it filled with deep dread
> Of following in that love the path others tread?
> Perhaps; among those of the past and today
> None was less trite and none more blasé.[7]

Among those budding writers Baudelaire met and with whom he set up a fruitful rivalry was the precocious poet Théodore de Banville, who published his first volume of poems, *Les Cariatides*, when he was only eighteen. When, many years later, he looked back at this time in their life, no doubt through glasses tinged with nostalgia, Baudelaire was to write: 'Paris, in those days, was not what it has become . . . a Babel populated with the imbecilic and the useless, who have little delicacy about ways of passing time and are completely rebellious to the pleasures of literature. In those days, the elite of Paris consisted of that select group of men charged with forming the opinion of the rest and who when a poet happened to be born were always the first to be advised of it' (*oc*, II, p. 162).

An exchange of sonnets written in the spring of 1845, together with an essay devoted to Banville's work that Baudelaire published in 1861, suggest why Baudelaire was aware of the need for that patience he mentioned to his mother. In his article he pays tribute to his friend's precocity but adds: 'his work as a whole, with its radiance and its variety, did not at first reveal the particular nature of its author, either because that nature was not yet sufficiently formed or because the poet was still under the fascinating charm of all the great poets of the age' (*oc*, II, pp. 162–3). And an age of great poets it certainly was, with Victor Hugo, Alphonse de Lamartine, Alfred de Musset and Théophile Gautier among others casting their enormous shadows over what Baudelaire would later refer to as the vast domain of poetry. Baudelaire, for his part, seems determined not to remain subject to that charm and to affirm from the outset his own 'particular nature'.

In 1845 Baudelaire wrote a sonnet for Banville, whose poetry he was later to describe as representing 'the happy hours' (*oc*, I, p. 656), 'the hours when you feel happy to think and to live' (*oc*, II, p. 163). It is a sonnet that not only shows the young poet's mastery of that form with its change of subject between quatrains and tercets, the power of his vocabulary and the originality of his images, but also indicates the yawning gulf between Banville's concept of what poetry was and Baudelaire's own far bleaker and more distinctive idea of it:

> You've seized the goddess by her curls,
> With a wrist as strong and just the air
> Of mastery and of devil may care,
> Of a ruffian throwing down his girl (*oc*, I, p. 208)

he asserts, with the blend of myth and modernity that would become typical of him. But even in this sonnet he suggests that his friend's combination of audacity and correctness of form merely hints at what he might become in later years. Correctness of form is not in itself beauty, for as Baudelaire affirms in his diaries, 'what is not slightly misshapen seems insensitive, from which it follows that irregularity, that is, the unexpected, surprise and astonishment, are an essential part of beauty and characteristic of it' (*oc*, I, p. 656).

Yet there is more, as the tercets reveal: 'Poet,' he insists, flattering him by giving him this accolade before revealing the chasm between them: 'our blood escapes through every pore'. It is an image he will pick up again in one of the poems included in *Les Fleurs du Mal*, 'The Fountain of Blood': 'It seems to me sometimes the blood spurts from my veins, / Like a fountain that in rhythmic pulses complains' (*oc*, I, p. 115). Poetry, for Baudelaire, would not be exclusively about the happy hours, but would show the fugitive nature of joy and indicate how even the gifts we receive, the momentary pleasures we enjoy, are steeped in poison, like the cloak that the centaur's wife unwittingly gave him and that destroyed him. It is that sharp awareness of the destructive nature of pleasure that creates such a contrast with Banville's own far more optimistic nature. Despite that difference, and despite their rivalry over Marie Daubrun, the actress known as 'the golden-haired beauty', the two poets remained friends for the rest of Baudelaire's life.

Another of his friends may well have suggested different possibilities to him: a lanky Guadeloupan, Alexandre Privat d'Anglemont went through his fortune even faster than Baudelaire did. Forced to earn a precarious living from journalism, he turned his quizzical gaze on the city's outcasts and pariahs, on those who lived from hand to mouth, or those whose work and indeed existence went largely unnoticed by the mass of the bourgeoisie. In addition to what he termed a prose quadrille, *La Closerie des lilas* of 1848, he published a collection of articles under the title *Paris anecdote* in 1854, and after his death his friends gathered another anthology under the title *Paris inconnu*. Baudelaire, aware of the dangers of publishing before his work was ready, seems to have collaborated closely enough with Privat for several of the sonnets that appeared above Privat's signature to be in fact Baudelaire's own, while others included in *La Closerie des lilas* may have been written by the two friends working together. Although Privat's journalistic prose style, which, like that of many of his contemporaries, lacked both muscle and fire, had little to offer to his younger friend, the glance he turned on the city and its inhabitants may well have sharpened Baudelaire's own sense of potential subjects. An irregular sonnet which initially appeared in *La Closerie des lilas* is not unlike some of Baudelaire's, especially in its rejection of standard Romantic images of female beauty. Loosely paraphrased it runs:

> I love her great blue eyes, her blazing hair with its strange per-
> fumes, her lovely body, pink and white, and her robust health.
> I love her proud gaze and her indecent dress that lets you see
> the curves of her abundant breasts, admired by sculptors. I love
> her bad taste, her brightly coloured skirt, her torn shawl, her
> wild speech and her low brow. So what if I love her like that!
> This girl of the streets sends me wild and fascinates me with
> her crude beauty. Too bad, I love her like that![8]

Another of these collaborations is closer still both in theme and style to poems that Baudelaire would eventually publish. Its title, 'To a Young Street Performer' recalls his fascination with street theatre in all its guises:

> We loved you well back then, when on your poignant harp
> You scratched out a romance, and gathered in the crowd

At crossroads where you'd leap just like a spawning carp,
While a scrofulous young boy would beat the drum out loud;

You'd twirl your scarf and ogle some leotarded athlete,
A well-built Hercules, the puny burgher's idol –
A crook whom the police would dearly love to hassle –
Who'd hoist a hundred kilos and call you his little sweetmeat.

Your rusty-voiced guitar, your skirt with all its spangles,
Spread out beneath our eyes the dreams of all the minstrels,
Hoffmann's ballerina, Esmeralda and sweet Mignon.

But then you fell from grace, and so our former angel,
Sultana of the street, in mud must grope and grovel,
For money that will go to booze for your companion.
(*oc*, I, pp. 221–2)

There are traces of other collaborations, most notably a sketch
for a play, *Idéolus*, which Baudelaire and Prarond appear to have
worked on together in the mid-1840s. Theatre in the nineteenth
century attracted many writers, who saw in it a path to fame and
fortune. Balzac, Stendhal and Mallarmé, to mention only three,
all tried their hand at writing for the stage. Throughout his life
Baudelaire was to have a string of theatre projects, none of which
came to much, although, as Marie Maclean argues in her remarkable study, *Narrative as Performance*, the demands and concepts
of the theatre underpin the structure of many of his prose poems.
In a letter to Eugène Crépet written some 40 years later, Prarond
asserted that the two friends planned to create a drama together,
in which one of the principal characters would be a philosophical
drunkard while another would be a sculptor, Idéolus, struggling
with the difficulties of creating art, and torn, as so many romantic
heroes were torn, between the lurid attractions of a whore, here the

well-named Forniquette, and the far worthier love of a good woman, here the equally well-named Nubilis. Much is made of the artist toiling to transform marble into art, the ineffectual efforts of 'the impotent artist who seeks to make his own blood flow into the stone' (*oc*, i, p. 621). Despite some moments of high melodrama, the projected ending – 'sale of the statues. *Deux ex machina*. Marriage' (*oc*, i, p. 605) – would probably not have come any too soon for the audience. The draft that remains closes at the end of act two with these words: 'Devil take it, my beauty! / So you've learnt the art of being rebellious to duty?' (*oc*, i, p. 626). Being rebellious to duty was not something Baudelaire seems to have had to learn, but it is hard to see in this outline any real indication of theatrical talent.

In 1843 Prarond, Le Vavasseur and August Dozon, the last of whom used the pen-name Argon, published a joint collection of poems to which Baudelaire had been invited to contribute. Indeed, according to Le Vavasseur, he had even supplied a manuscript consisting of early drafts of some of the poems which would later appear in *Les Fleurs du mal*. But faced with Le Vavasseur's critical suggestion, the young poet calmly withdrew his manuscript. Looking back at this incident in 1886 Le Vavasseur wrote: 'This was the right decision for him. His new, harsh material, in which the impurities were deliberately woven into the cloth, was of an entirely different nature from our calico.'⁹ If it was obvious that Baudelaire even then could brook no criticism of his work, it is also likely that he realized that he would do better to wait, reserving his fire until he was ready to reveal more than the squibs of these early drafts. As another of his friends from that period, Jules Buisson, asserted, using the imagery of *Les Fleurs du mal*: 'He did not want to let any scent escape from his perfume flask before he had filled it. What he needed was a volume entirely to himself.'¹⁰

Meanwhile, Baudelaire sought other ways of carrying out his determination to be a writer. However much he might despise the hack journalist, the prestige of art criticism certainly exerted an appeal. In 1845 he wrote a review of that year's art salon, publishing it in a 72-page pamphlet, the cover of which optimistically announced that another of the author's works, *On Modern Painting*, was in print, while a third, *On Caricature*, was soon to appear. Neither work was anywhere near as ready as this suggests, but then, throughout his life Baudelaire would have trouble differentiating between conception and completion: 'certainly', he would assert in one of the poems included in the 'Revolt' section of *Les Fleurs du mal*, 'I will be happy to leave a world in which action is not the sister of dream' (*oc*, I, p. 122).

His account of the 1845 salon appeared over the pen-name he had chosen for himself, inspired by his mother's maiden name: Baudelaire Dufaÿs, with a somewhat archaic and pretentious *tréma* over the y. After trying a range of variations on that name, he would abandon it, and given the number of critics and publishers who struggled even with the correct spelling of Baudelaire, sneaking in that extra 'e' in the first syllable that enraged its owner, it is probably as well that he set aside anything as complex as Dufaÿs.

Baudelaire's love of painting had received an injection of vitality on 9 March 1845 with the publication in the periodical *L'Artiste* of an account of the 1759 Salon by the Enlightenment polymath Denis Diderot. As Gita May has shown, the young writer benefited considerably from his reading of Diderot's text, with its powerful and above all personal appreciation of the works of art displayed. In a letter to Champfleury, Baudelaire urged his friend 'if he wanted to give him pleasure' to mention Diderot's 'Salon' when reviewing Baudelaire's. Champfleury did indeed do so, writing anonymously in the *Corsaire-Satan* of 27 May 1845: 'This little volume is a curiosity, an eccentricity, a truth. M. Baudelaire-Dufaÿs is as bold as Diderot, except for the paradox. There is much in it that recalls Stendhal, the two men who have written best about painting.'[11] The meticulous corrections Baudelaire made to Asselineau's preface to his work, *La Double Vie*, suggest that the sloppiness of Champfleury's sentence structure here would have made the young poet sneer, but the comparison with Diderot and Stendhal would certainly have given him pleasure. Both Stendhal's art criticism and his tongue-in-cheek treatise on love attracted Baudelaire's enthusiasm, and an echo of his claim that he wrote for the 'happy few' can be found in the younger writer's affirmation in the 'Salon of 1845' that 'we know we will be understood by few, but that is enough for us' (*oc*, II, p. 357). As for Diderot, the conversational rhythms as well as the highly personal tone of his art criticism find a clear echo in Baudelaire's. Baudelaire picks up this tone and embroiders on it in, for instance, his comment on Robert Fleury: 'Robert Fleury continues to be always the same, that is, a very good and curious painter. Without exactly having outstanding merit and, if I can put it like this, without a kind of involuntary genius like the great masters, he has all you can get from willpower and good taste' (*oc*, II, p. 363).

Indeed, even at this early stage in his career, his account of the Salon of 1845 reveals much about Baudelaire's skills as a writer. Always a master of the gripping opening sentence or paragraph, he chooses to begin with a statement guaranteed to arrest the attention: 'We can say with at least as much truth as a well-known writer about his own little books: what we write, the newspapers will not dare to print' (*oc*, II, p. 351). The 'well-known writer' was the journalist Alphonse Karr who throughout the 1840s published a series of anecdotes under the title 'The Wasps'. Unlike Karr's cruel insolence, however, Baudelaire's 'Salon', so he claims, would prove unprintable for the opposite reason: his impartiality. According to the tyro critic, everyone else writing about the Salon was driven by personal friendships or enmities, making the middle-class readers disgusted with the reviews, despite their usefulness as guides to the exhibition. For his part, Baudelaire claimed to set out full of scorn for all systematic grumbling, with a love of order and good sense and a determination to talk about everything that drew the eyes of the crowd and of artists. In this early 'Salon' there is little of the broader argument about colour and schools that dominates the later reviews, but there is already the marked admiration for Delacroix that runs all through Baudelaire's writing, shaping his thinking about painting and influencing many of the poems both in subject matter and in choice of imagery. Drawn to Delacroix for his energetic depictions of contemporary as well as mythological and historical themes and for his intense use of colour to suggest not just shape but also mood, Baudelaire found in him a hero who always remained somewhat aloof, but from whom he would cull a series of ideas that were central to his thinking.

Baudelaire opens the section of his 'Salon of 1845' that focuses on historical paintings with a belligerent judgement in which the painter of *Liberty Leading the People* and *The Women of Algiers* is hyperbolically described as 'decidedly the most original painter of antiquity and the modern day' (*oc*, II, p. 353), a genius incessantly searching for something new. What is remarkable is the extent to which this study points forward to Baudelaire's later writing, where he deals at greater length and more suavely with certain issues that are raised here with the impatience and brevity of youth. Delacroix's command of colour, the emphasis he places on green and red, his skill at suggesting outlines through colour rather than line, all these details that Baudelaire will develop in later art criticism are touched on briefly here, making the great master of Romanticism appear much closer than one might have suspected to Constantin Guys, the 'painter of modern life' whose work Baudelaire explores some two decades later.

To read this account of the Salon is to overhear the conversation between Baudelaire, his painter friend Deroy and the young critic Asselineau, who had just met the two others for the first time. There is a liveliness and intensity about it, a lack of either respect or familiarity that gives it freshness and an assuredness of touch that dominates the writing despite the rather unimaginative way in which the painters are discussed more or less in the order in which a visitor to the Salon might encounter them. Most importantly, perhaps, the account of the Salon closes on what is a highly condensed affirmation of artistic faith. Let's note, the young critic argues, that 'everyone paints better and better, which strikes us as a cause for despair. But where invention, ideas, temperament are concerned there's not a jot more than there was before' (*oc*, II, p. 407). These three elements – originality, the imaginative force behind a work and the artist's ability to convey his or her temperament, their personal view of the world – are those that Baudelaire will continue to emphasize. Rejecting the contemporary argument between colour and line, he adds, in a passage that is even more important in indicating the direction in which his own ambitions are moving:

> No one is listening to the wind that will blow tomorrow, and yet the heroism *of modern life* surrounds us and presses down on us . . . The true painter will be the one who knows how to seize the epic side of contemporary life and make us see and understand, with colour or line, how great and poetic we are in our cravats and our polished boots. Let us hope that next year the real seekers give us that special joy of being able to celebrate the arrival of the *new*. (*oc*, II, p. 407)

The joint determination and ability to show the heroism of modern life and to reveal what was new and striking under its familiarity runs through much of his subsequent writing.

However pleased Baudelaire may have been with the publication of this pamphlet, the difficult realities of his complex existence were not to be calmed by such intellectual and aesthetic gestures. On 30 June 1845, shortly after writing his account of the Salon,

Baudelaire sent a letter to Ancelle via Jeanne Duval. It began with the dramatic lines: 'By the time [Jeanne] gives you this letter I will be dead. She does not know this' (*c*, I, p. 124). He went on to explain that he was killing himself, not because of his debts (nothing is easier to dominate than such matters, claimed the man who never managed to dominate them), but because 'the weariness of going to sleep and waking up again have become unbearable to me' (*c*, I, p. 124). Much later, the poet's erstwhile friend, Louis Ménard, would dismiss this as no more than a romantic gesture, but by that stage he had become estranged from Baudelaire, in part because of the latter's somewhat mocking review of his book, *Prométhée délivré*, which appeared in February 1846. In that review, Baudelaire, having depicted *Prométhée délivré* as philosophical poetry, goes on to affirm that this is a false genre, and he accuses Ménard of being unaware of the value of 'strongly coloured rhymes, those lanterns that illuminate the path the idea follows' (*oc*, II, p. 110).

Whatever the truth behind the suicide gesture, Baudelaire's letters of the time suggest the physical difficulties and discomforts of his life: incessantly dunned by his creditors, constantly begging his mother and Ancelle for money, changing lodgings at short notice and at times unable to go outside; either because he feared meeting the police or because he didn't have enough clean linen. These experiences leave an unmistakable mark on such prose poems as 'The Double Room' with its depiction of 'dusty, chipped furniture', 'its fireplace bereft of flame and embers', its sad windows down which 'rain has drawn furrows in the dust', its 'manuscripts, scratched through and incomplete', its 'almanac on which the pencil has marked the sinister dates' (*oc*, I, p. 281). Here, the prose poem claims, you breathe in the dank stench of despondency. It is a smell that lingers over many of Baudelaire's poems, especially in the 'Spleen' section of *Les Fleurs du mal*. The first 'Spleen' poem, for instance, creates a sharply observed combination of the sights, smells and sounds that build the universe of melancholy and boredom that seems so suddenly to have become Baudelaire's lot. January, he asserts, using the wonderful Revolutionary name for the month, Pluviôse, the rainy one, angry with the entire city, pours darkness and cold from his great urn onto the pale ghosts of the nearby graveyard, while mortality rains down on the foggy suburbs. The thin mangy cat, seeking a bed on the tiled floor, moves about unceasingly. The soul of an old poet wanders in the down pipe with the sad voice of a shivering phantom. The great bell mourns, and the smoking log accompanies in falsetto the sniffling clock while, in a malodorous pack, the fatal inheritance of a dropsical old woman, the handsome knave of hearts and the queen of spades chat in sinister tones about a passion long since spent.

But that of course was not the whole story: Baudelaire's nature is so complex that he also found the energy to write for the anti-establishment newspaper *Le Corsaire-Satan* an exuberant parody inspired by Balzac and bearing the title 'How to pay your debts when you are a genius'. 'If anyone were to take this as an attack on the glory of the greatest man of our age, he would be shamefully mistaken', Baudelaire wrote when he came to republish this article a few months later. 'I wanted to show that the great poet knew how to deal with a demand for payment just as easily as with the most mysterious and highly plotted novel' (*oc*, ii, p. 8). Unfortunately the device the great man employs in this parody was not available to Baudelaire. It requires having a name so well known that you can demand an advance payment large enough to let you hire hacks to do the actual writing for you.

At least, however, Baudelaire could earn some money by pub-lishing a review of an exhibition mounted by the museum that had been created in the store known as the Bazaar Bonne-Nouvelle. Since 1842 this vast establishment had become highly popular with Parisians both for its range of products for sale, from chocolates and cigars to clothing, and for its picture gallery. Most importantly for

Baudelaire, the great painter Ingres, who since 1834 had consistently refused to exhibit in the annual Salons, had agreed to display eleven of his paintings at the Bazaar's museum in order to promote the charitable works of the philanthropist Baron Taylor, in this case on behalf of indigent artists. In addition there were ten works by Louis David, including *The Assassination of Marat*, as well as a large array of works by other artists, both established and less well known.

The exhibition opened in the first days of January 1846 and Baudelaire for once was quick off the mark, publishing his article on the twenty-first of that month. His excitement and pleasure at the chance to see these works leap out at us from his opening sentences: 'Every thousand years, someone has a bright idea. We should count ourselves lucky, therefore, that the year 1846 was among those allotted us, for 1846 has given to sincere lovers of art the pleasure of ten canvases by David and eleven by Ingres' (*oc*, II, p. 408). He draws a telling comparison between the bustle of the Salons and the tranquillity reigning at the Bazaar's exhibition: 'our annual exhibitions, with their turbulence, their noise, their violence and their pushing and shoving, cannot give any idea of this exhibition, which is as calm, gentle and serious as a place of study'. Calm, gentle and serious Baudelaire's article was certainly not, since it resembles nothing so much as an exuberant firework display. After that excited opening statement, he moves into a spirited questioning of the notion of charity and its logical consequences, then gives a scintillating overview of the paintings on display before closing with a passage devoted to bourgeois appreciation of art, a topic he will raise again in his 'Salon of 1846'. He opens with an ironic question: since this exhibition is, after all, being held to benefit the poor, what does one do with the poor who demand a reduction on the ticket price, and who have to be turned away on the grounds that as they are not artists they are not the right sort of poor?

Baudelaire closes his review with a paragraph which, with its attack on bourgeois artists who place the blame for their lack of sales on bourgeois hatred of all that is fine and good, glitters with slippery irony. No doubt inspired by the mercantile nature of the Bazaar, Baudelaire argues that the grocer is a great thing, for, by eating up the academic painter Léon Cogniet, he proves that he possesses enormous stocks of good will. Serve him a masterpiece, Baudelaire argues, and he will digest it and be all the better for it. That Baudelaire had expressed admiration for one of Cogniet's portraits in the 1845 Salon merely makes this little dig all the more difficult to interpret, but Asselineau may be correct when he comments that such attacks were written, 'not as one might believe through a love of paradox, but through hatred of the half-bourgeois and the false artist'[12] and above all in a desire to go directly to his main readership, side-stepping what he was to call in the 'Salon of 1846' 'the distributors of praise and blame', the professional critics who tell the bourgeoisie they have no right to feel and to enjoy on their own behalf but need to be told what values they should uphold (*oc*, II, p. 415). Perhaps. With Baudelaire it is often hard to tell where the irony begins and ends. In the notes titled *Fusées* he identifies 'two fundamental literary qualities: supernaturalism and irony' (*oc*, I, p. 658).

Baudelaire's enthusiasm for art was not so all-consuming that it stilled his critical sense, heightened in any case by the constant witticisms produced by the group who wrote for the *Corsaire-Satan*, the little newspaper whose offices he frequented at this time. His opening salvo in response to the 1846 Salon would be a short, anonymous volume produced in concert with his friends Théodore de Banville and Auguste Vitu, in which 60 caricatures, each with a rhyming caption, took aim at the Salon jury, the press, the public, the exhibitors, the exhibited and the paintings themselves. The press is depicted as a baby in a walker, above the lines: 'in the virginal guise of this one-year-old tot / criticism loudly demands grub – a lot!' while the public is represented by a gormless young man described in the following tones: 'This young subscriber to the *Epoque* / Finds the Salon highly baroque, / Giggles and snuffles like a cock' (*oc*, II, p. 502). And so forth. While no masterpiece, this little volume does bear tribute to Baudelaire's fascination with caricature, and sheds some light, however diffuse, on his sense of humour. It also provides a counterpoint to the bleakness of the letters written at this stage, indicating that in coffee-houses like the Divan Le Peletier and in the offices of newspapers like the *Corsaire-Satan* Baudelaire enjoyed the pleasures of friendship and set aside the dark melancholy that dominates the tone of his correspondence.

By May 1846 Baudelaire was writing his more formal assessment of the art salon, in a far more original and imaginative appreciation than his 'Salon of 1845' had been. As if continuing the debate concerning the role of the bourgeois in art, begun in his account of the exhibition at the Bazaar, he opens this study with an extended dedication to the middle classes. In this dedication he begins building up the portrait of the ideal viewer, the ideal reader that he wants for art and literature. 'Enjoyment is a science, and the exercise of the five senses demands a particular initiation, which comes about by good will and necessity' (*oc*, II, p. 415). Artists, Baudelaire asserts pragmatically, need patrons, just as writers need people who buy books: only the bourgeoisie can do this. And so, he concludes, perhaps tongue-in-cheek, perhaps cynically, this book is dedicated to them, 'because any book that is not addressed to the majority – in terms of numbers and intelligence – is a stupid book' (*oc*, II, p. 417). Asselineau affirms that this account of the Salon assured Baudelaire's reputation as a writer within the circle of his peers and his friends, but the wider public, whether or not it was ready to devour Baudelaire as it had Cogniet, seems to have remained largely unaware of the book so generously dedicated to it.

Baudelaire's 'Salon of 1846' is a far more mature work than the analysis of the 1845 Salon: it is not only organized thematically rather than artist by artist, thus allowing Baudelaire to drive his points home in a more forceful and unified manner, but it is also both underpinned and driven forward by a particular polemic, a specific vision of what art and art criticism might be. And already he appears to revel in the possibility of drawing on a combination of art forms usually considered disparate: thus, in exploring the scientific causes of colour, he affirms that colour, which creates the great 'symphony of the day', includes harmony, melody and counterpoint (*oc*, ii, p. 423).

In addition to an idiosyncratic but highly informed exploration of contemporary painting and sculpture, Baudelaire's assessment of the Salon is remarkable for his lucid questioning of the role of criticism and for his attempt to define Romanticism, still the prevalent artistic movement in France at that time. The technical details of how a work is produced do not lie within the critic's domain, according to Baudelaire, just as later he will ask, truculently: 'Do you bring the crowd into the studio?' (*oc*, i, p. 185). For Baudelaire, what criticism demands is an impassioned response to the results of the means and procedures employed, a response that enters as deeply as possible into the artist's temperament and that acknowledges that the great artist is the one who blends what is intrinsic to his or her nature with the most recent and modern expression of beauty. It is that stress on the modern image of beauty that leads him into his exploration of Romanticism, as he defines it. Above all, he argues, Romanticism is the most recent expression of beauty, springing from a sharp aware-ness of what the modern world has to offer that makes its forms of beauty unique. 'Romanticism,' he affirms, 'is modern art – that is, intimacy, spirituality, colour, an aspiration to the infinite, expressed through all the means that the arts contain' (*oc*, ii, p. 421). However little he has in common with earlier French Romantics like Hugo and Lamartine, Baudelaire would continue to see himself as 'an old Romantic'. But to understand that claim we need to remember that what he saw as Romanticism was above all an intensely felt and powerfully expressed response to the modern world, seized in all its transience, colour and complexity.

As if to reveal something of what such a theory might lead to in terms of theoretical writing, Baudelaire devotes a section of his 'Salon' to colour. In much of his critical writing it is clear that Baudelaire is flexing his writing muscles by accepting a challenge some other creative figure has thrown down to him: Hugo's power to write about the sea, Marceline Desbordes-Valmore's transformation of nature into emotional states or Delacroix's manipulation of colour to create feeling can all stimulate him to try his hand at outdoing them in his own medium. The same would be true when he turned to translating. In the passage titled 'On colour', a passage his English biographer Enid Starkie justifiably described as a prose poem, he seems to have in mind the kind of effects Delacroix can create by a powerful and suggestive use of colour.

Let's imagine a lovely natural space where everything gleams in gold and red, where dust motes dance and light glimmers in complete freedom, where everything, differently coloured according to its molecular constitution, changes from second to second the movement of light and shade, and as a result of the heat within it, moves ceaselessly, making the lines tremble and fulfilling the law of eternal and universal movement. An immense area, sometimes blue but mostly green, stretches to the edge of the sky: this is the sea. The trees are green, the grass is green, the mosses are green; the colour green snakes through the trunks, the young wood is green; green is the basis of nature because green blends so easily with all the other colours. What strikes me first is that everywhere, whether it is poppies in the grass or parrots etc., red sings the glory of green; black – when there is any – is a solitary and insignificant cipher that intercedes on behalf of blue or red. The blue, that is, the sky is broken by light white flakes or grey masses that felicitously dilute its bleak crudeness, and, like the mist specific to the season whether it be summer or winter, bathes, softens or envelops the contours, so that nature recalls a top, which, spinning ever faster, appears to us as grey, even though it contains all the colours.

Eugène Delacroix, *Women of Algiers in their Room*, 1834, oil on canvas.

The sap rises and because it blends the principal colours, glows
in mixed tones; the trees, rocks, and granite stones are mirrored in
the water and leave their reflections in it; all the transparent
objects seize light and colour as they pass close at hand or far off.
As the day star moves across the scene the tones change in value,
but, always respecting their mutual sympathies and antipathies,
continue to live in harmony with each other through a series of
reciprocal concessions. The shadows move slowly by, driving the
tones before them or snuffing them out as the light, which moves
in parallel, seeks to bring out new tones. (*oc*, II, p. 423)

The passage is fascinating not just for its determination to analyse
the relationships among light and colours and to do so in a way
that rivals the beauty of a painted representation, but also for its –
perhaps too obvious – attempt to understand the physical reasons
for these changes. If Balzac, that great painter of modern life, drew

inspiration from science in his classification of his characters, so the young poet seems here to look to the science of colour to stiffen the sinews of his art criticism.

In addition to its close analysis of Delacroix, the great exponent of colour, and Ingres, the master of line, together with their followers, the 'Salon' also offers some remarkable – and ambitious – theoretical statements. Central among these is the role of memory. Art, Baudelaire argues, is a device for remembering beauty (*oc*, II, p. 455) and he clarifies his statement by affirming that mere imitation spoils beauty by failing to transform it through the filtering power of the artist's personality. This becomes particularly clear in regard to portrait painting, which Baudelaire says can be understood either as history or as a novel, by which he means either as a truthful representation of an external, if idealized, truth or an imaginative reconstruction of inner truth. His discussion of the second method is worth quoting at length because it sheds light on his own technique as a creative writer:

> The second method, which is specific to the colourists, consists in making the portrait into a painting, a poem with its accessories,

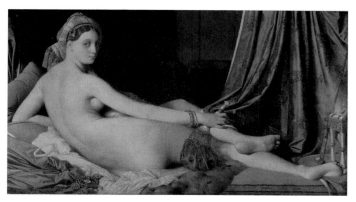

Jean-Auguste-Dominique Ingres, *Odalisque*, 1814, oil on canvas.

full of space and dream. Here the art is more difficult because it is more ambitious. You have to be able to bathe a head in the gentle vapours of a hot atmosphere or make it rise from the depths of dusk. Here imagination plays a great role and yet, just as it often happens that the novel is truer than history, it can also be the case that a model is more clearly expressed through the generous and free-flowing brush of a colourist than through the pencil of the line specialist. (*oc*, ii, p. 465)

As Whistler would say later: it takes years for a man to look like his portrait. Revealing individuals against the background that shapes them, either physically or metaphorically, is one of the poet's skills, too, as we can see most powerfully, perhaps, in the section of *Les Fleurs du mal* devoted to Paris and in many of the prose poems.

The following year Baudelaire himself would once more be the subject of a portrait, that of Courbet. This portrait shows a very different Baudelaire from the one depicted by Deroy. No longer the flamboyantly dressed young man with long locks, looking directly out at us from the canvas, as he lolls at ease in an arm chair, this one wears his hair cut short and is far more self-contained. While he is still stylishly dressed and sports a flowing cravat, and while there is a degree of vanity in the beautiful hand he displays for us, this is much more a portrait of a thinker. He is lost in a dog-eared book, which he leans against a desk on which stands, ready for his inspiration, a long white quill. The light gleams on his slightly balding brow and intensifies the sense of brooding concentration. This is a head that rises from the 'depths of dusk' as Baudelaire wrote in the 'Salon', forcing our attention not by the direct gaze Baudelaire used in the Deroy portrait but by the intellectual force suggested by the hidden gaze.

Like the 'Salon of 1845', that of 1846 closes with another impassioned call to artists to reveal the heroism of modern life. It's here that Baudelaire begins to express what will be a long-held belief,

Gustave Courbet, *Baudelaire*, 1847/8, oil on canvas.

that 'all beauty contains, like all possible phenomena, something eternal and something transient, something absolute and something particular' (*oc*, II, p. 493). What lends it its charm and its intensity is that particular element that comes from individual passions. 'Parisian life,' he asserts, 'is fertile in poetic and wonderful subjects. The wonderful envelopes us and sustains us like the atmosphere but we do not see it' (*oc*, II, p. 496).

What was enveloping Baudelaire and his fellow-citizens in these years was a very different kind of atmosphere, that of the political turbulence and social unrest that would lead to the end of the French monarchy. These were years when many thinkers were producing visions of utopian societies that would transform the categories that appeared entrenched in French society. Such utopian visions aroused much enthusiasm among many of the great Romantic writers, and Baudelaire was briefly swept up in that general enthusiasm. Louis-Philippe's government had become increasingly conservative, unaware or unmindful of the disaffection of the majority of its citizens. The radical groups had been forced underground as a result of various edicts known as the September laws, but this repression led only to the spawning of a large number of secret societies, each promoting its own blend of utopian thinking. Gustave Flaubert would offer his own sardonic view of some of these groups in his novel *L'Education sentimentale*. At the same time, an economic depression led to considerable suffering in both the agricultural and industrial sectors. The leaders of the opposition, Adolphe Thiers and Odilon Barrot, moved their campaign outside parliament, promoting a series of banquets at which speakers urged electoral reform and an end to government corruption. When the government prohibited what would have been the largest of these, planned for 22 February 1848, passions exploded into such civil unrest that Louis-Philippe was forced to abdicate, and for the second time in French history the insistent demands of the populace led to the proclamation of a republic.

The revolution of 1848, and the heady months that led up to it, inspired the excitement and stirred the imaginations of many of the young writers at the time, from Leconte de Lisle and Champfleury to Baudelaire and the worker poet whose songs he would help promote, Pierre Dupont. Looking back at this period from the far bleaker time when he came to write his intimate diaries, Baudelaire seems bemused by the excitement these events aroused in him. 'My intoxication in 1848,' he writes, 'what was the nature of that intoxication?' And he adds succinctly: 'A taste for vengeance. A *natural* pleasure in demolition' (*oc*, I, p. 679). It is, he indicates, a legitimate taste, if everything that is natural is legitimate. But, as he insists elsewhere in the diaries, what is natural is abominable, far removed from the control and willed artifice of the dandy. Part of it at least he blames on his reading: 'a literary intoxication. The memory of books read.' He was far from being alone in this realization of the yawning gap between reading and life, between the imagined utopia and the unvarnished reality of violence. George Sand's involvement in the utopian movement had been deeper and more intellectually profound than his, and the shock she experienced at the realization that only by extreme violence could change come about sent her back to the country, where for some time she withdrew from social life to concentrate on creating utopias in her novels.

Another passage in the diaries is far more desolate in its suggestion of what Baudelaire had come to realize about the nature of society, in part as a direct result of the 1848 revolution and its longer-term results.

> It is not too hard for our imaginations to conceive republics and other communal states, worthy of some glory, if they are led by noble men, by certain aristocrats. But it is not really through political institutions that universal ruin or universal progress . . . will be revealed. That will come about through the debasement of the heart. (*oc*, i, p. 666)

These notes end abruptly with Baudelaire's assertion that what he has written has been a mere sidetrack, but he adds, with a telling hesitation between two words: 'Nevertheless, I'll leave these pages – because I want to mark my anger / sorrow' (*oc*, i, p. 667). This was no doubt written much later in Baudelaire's life, and while the anger belongs more to his earlier years and the sorrow to a later period, the passage bears the unmistakable mark of his experiences in 1848.

Even then, the anger the young writer felt seems to have been directed less at the government than at his own personal demons, above all his step-father. On 24 February 1848, the day when another poet, Alphonse de Lamartine, went before the people to ask it to ratify the new republic, Baudelaire was seen brandishing a rifle and

shouting 'We must shoot General Aupick. Down with Aupick!' A
letter written to his mother late in 1847 helps set the context for
that outburst of purely personal rage. A curious but typical mixture
of begging, self-incrimination and self-justification, the letter, however exaggerated and histrionic, nevertheless conveys something of
the irritation, ambition and desperation Baudelaire was experienc-
ing at the time. 'My idleness is destroying me, devouring me,
eating me up,' he confesses (*c*, I, p. 143). 'I don't know,' he boasts,
'how I possess enough strength to dominate the disastrous effects
of that idleness, and still possess an absolute lucidity of mind as
well as a perpetual hope for fortune, happiness and calm.' The fact
is, he continues, 'I have been living for several months in a supernatural state of mind.' The coming months would only exacerbate
that mood, but Baudelaire had, he told his mother, formed a plan,
one that was 'excessively simple'. He would complete the two articles he had been asked to write some eight months ago and that
he had still not completed, his history of caricature and a history
of sculpture. 'For me,' he adds, 'such matters are a mere game.'
Perhaps, but while the study of caricature was eventually completed
and published, no study devoted to sculpture was ever finished,
although it may have been incorporated into his later art writing.
But there is more: 'Starting on New Year's Day, I am beginning a
new career – the creation of works of pure imagination, Novels. I
don't need to demonstrate to you here the gravity and beauty, and
the infinite dimension of that art. As we are speaking of material
questions, all you need to know is that *good or bad, everything can be
sold*; you need only be assiduous.' But assiduity was not something
Baudelaire could display, for reasons that concern both his personal
position and the wider political atmosphere. The paucity of letters
and documents from these years make it difficult to follow him
closely, but clearly the bitter memories they left him cast a pall that
adds its bleak trace in the intensity of his response to the violence
of revolution.

The word Baudelaire used for his feelings in early 1848 was intoxication, *ivresse*, a term he would take up in a prose poem in which he urges his readers, if they do not want to be the martyred slaves of time, to remain always intoxicated, on wine, poetry or virtue as they choose. Anger seems to have been the main source of his intoxication during these months. By May, the intransigent problem of unemployment, which the new republican government had tried to resolve by the establishment of national workshops, provoked mass protests, leading in late June to bloody street fighting and a vicious anti-populist reaction. And it provided the justification the reactionaries had been seeking. They invited Napoleon's nephew Louis to become the president of the French Republic. At this period, according to Gustave Le Vavasseur, Baudelaire, profoundly and irrationally excited, was closely aligned with forces of the left, but assessing it with hindsight he would refer to 'the horrors of June. Madness of the people and madness of the bourgeoisie. A natural love of crime' (*oc*, I, p. 679). Once again, the word *natural* offers its oblique but unmistakeable judgement. At the time, however, Baudelaire was writing to the political theorist Pierre-Joseph Proudhon, famous for his declaration that property was theft, warning him that he was in danger and clearly eager to meet him. The emotionalism of Baudelaire's letter is such that it is hardly surprising that Proudhon, not wishing to share Marat's fate, preferred to hear of the danger in a letter instead of at a face to face meeting with someone completely unknown to him. Baudelaire may also have been involved in some journalism for provincial newspapers, just as it is possible that he contemplated leaving France to find relief from the increasing harassment of his creditors. But what was becoming increasingly clear to him was, as he put it later on, that a 'monarchy or a republic based on democracy are equally absurd and weak' (*oc*, I, p. 684). When Louis Napoleon declared himself emperor after a *coup d'état* at the end of 1851, Baudelaire's fury appears to have been short lived. He proclaimed himself physically depoliticized, and whatever political or social convictions drove him now found their outlet not in actions but in his creative writing.

3

Second Empire Paris

A photograph by Nadar captures Baudelaire in the mid-1850s gazing warily out, tight-lipped and curious, as if he were watching the rapid transformation of his city and society. Indeed, the 1850s were years that saw profound changes in France, changes that affected the political situation of the country, the physical appearance of Paris and the constitution of the press. The Emperor Napoleon III's 20-year reign was marked by alternating periods of harsh repression and comparative liberalism, an emphasis on material prosperity, including an active social policy intended to mollify workers by improving their lot and, as a result of the Emperor's marriage to Eugénie de Montijo, a series of important concessions to the Catholic Church.

Determined not to be overthrown by yet another revolution, and equally certain that he wanted to continue the building projects of his uncle, Napoleon III set Baron Haussman in charge of an ambitious project of public works that would widen the narrow streets, thus making it more difficult to build barricades across them; provide larger vistas through the city, which would both beautify it and make it easier to police; and, by creating more housing for the middle and upper classes, would force the poorer population to move to the edges of the city where they posed less of a threat. What we now see as the classic heart of Paris is really a political programme written in stone. For Baudelaire and his contemporaries, however, large areas of central Paris were reduced for

Félix Nadar,
Charles Baudelaire,
1855.

most of the decade to a massive demolition and building site, a pile
of rubble that revealed how fragile even the apparent permanence
of great cities could be.

In addition, despite tight governmental control of the press,
the proliferation of short-lived periodicals in the years immediately
after the 1848 revolution continued under the Second Empire,
which also saw a flowering of new printing houses. The publishing
companies of Hachette, Lévy and Larousse all came into being
during these years, responding to the growing demand from an
increasingly literate population and opening up more possibilities
for writers and critics seeking to publish their work.

Among those ambitious publishers was a young man from the
provinces, Auguste Poulet-Malassis, whom Baudelaire first met
around the beginning of the decade and whose acquaintance, and

subsequently friendship, he cultivated with a care unusual for the often short-tempered and wilfully rebarbative poet. Obviously Baudelaire saw in Poulet-Malassis not only someone who could play an essential role in his plan to present his creative writing to the reading public but also a man whose aesthetic tastes had much in common with his own. Indeed, in the course of the decade Poulet-Malassis built up an astonishing and admirable list of publications, despite a series of fines levied on him for what was perceived as the morally pernicious or politically inflammatory content of some of those works. Among his stable of writers was Baudelaire's friend Théodore de Banville, who would capture him in one of his many witty rhymes:

> Malassis
> the editor
> whom silently, incessantly,
> all unpublished poets implore.[1]

Something of his personality can be detected in his choice of a publisher's symbol: a chicken (*poulet*) uncomfortably seated (*mal assis*) on a perch.

That Baudelaire had by this time gathered together a collection of poems he felt was ready for publication is suggested by the fact that in 1849 he planned to bring out a volume under the title *Les*

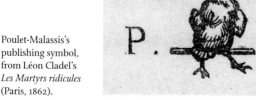

Poulet-Malassis's publishing symbol, from Léon Cladel's *Les Martyrs ridicules* (Paris, 1862).

Limbes (*Limbo*) on the anniversary of the February uprising, but, as was often the case with his projects, by 1850 it was still being announced as forthcoming. Nevertheless, in the summer of that year an anthology of love poetry organized by the journalist and publisher Julien Lemer included Baudelaire's poem 'Lesbos', one of those the 1857 tribunal was to ban. Through one of those revealing ironies of history, in Lemer's anthology Baudelaire's paean to passionate love was followed by an utterly banal sonnet entitled 'To a Creole Woman'. The last tercet of this sonnet can suffice: 'Yet yesterday, my lazy beauty / your hand forgot itself in my burning hand. / Do you regret it?'[2] The contrast with Baudelaire's powerful opening stanzas is telling, even in translation:

> Mother of Latin games, Mother of Greek pleasures,
> Lesbos, where kisses, pining and fervent,
> Adorn the long nights and the days of leisure,
> Warm as the sun, cool as a torrent,
> Mother of Latin games, Mother of Greek pleasures.
>
> Lesbos where kisses flow like cascades,
> Fearlessly plunging into bottomless chasms,
> Stormy and secret, copious and unafraid,
> Sobbing and moaning in unending spasms,
> Lesbos where kisses flow like cascades. (*oc*, I, p. 150)

In this rich and complex poem of outlawed passion, Baudelaire places physical love above heaven and hell, and boldly raises the question: 'What do the laws of the just and the unjust have to do with us?', a question asked twice through the stanza form in which the first line is repeated as the verse's fifth and final line.

Baudelaire's preconceptions about the nature of men and women, and particularly about the gendered nature of art, are clearly revealed in this poem where the great Greek poet Sappho is described as '*mâle*', virile, but she is also depicted as more beautiful than Venus because of the suffering love inflicts on her. 'I have found the definition of beauty, of my beauty', Baudelaire would write in his collection of jottings known as *Fusées*.

> It is something ardent and sad, something whose slight vagueness leaves room for conjecture . . . I am not claiming that Joy cannot be linked to Beauty, but I am saying that Joy is one of its most banal ornaments, whereas Melancholy is, so to speak, its illustrious companion, to the point where I can hardly conceive (is my brain a bewitched mirror?) of a kind of Beauty that does not include Unhappiness. (*oc*, I, pp. 657–8)

Sappho's power comes, in the poet's eyes, from the combination of grief, associated with the feminine, and genius, associated with the masculine, creating that blend of the sexes that he so admires in great writers, and to which he draws particular attention in his review of Flaubert's *Madame Bovary*.

Although Baudelaire was far from being alone in his interest in lesbian love – among several others, his friends Balzac and Gautier had preceded him, the first with *The Girl with the Golden Eyes* (1834–5) and the second with *Mademoiselle de Maupin* (1834) – his choice of this topic for one of his first published poems indicates his refusal to conform both to the growing prudishness of the age and to conventional literary images of women. Above all, however, he attributed to lesbians a longing similar to that of the insatiable Don Juan, for, as Baudelaire insisted in his brief sketch for an opera libretto based on that archetypical seducer, 'what creates pleasure is not the nature of the objects desired, but the energy of the desiring appetite' (*oc*, I, p. 638). It is not prurience but that energy of the desiring appetite, together with sorrow over the loss of innocence and a defiant refusal to accept banal reality, that dominates Baudelaire's poems about lesbians.

A similar rejection of the conventional images of women and of love can be found in another poem, 'The Ideal', first published in 1851 as part of *Les Limbes*. In this irregular sonnet he abruptly dismisses the Romantic image of the simpering and sickly heroine, replacing her with the powerful figures of Shakespeare's blood-stained Lady Macbeth and Michelangelo's potent Night. It is, moreover, not just the nature of woman that is at issue here, but Baudelaire's growing tendency to view life, at least in his poetry, through the lens of great literature or great art.

The combination of the filter through great art with that resounding rejection of current literary modes found a further expression when, towards the end of 1851, a group of friends led by the poet, novelist and food-lover Charles Monselet created a review, *La Semaine théâtrale*, in which Baudelaire published an acerbic essay ironically entitled 'Les Drames et les romans honnêtes' ('Honest Plays and Novels'). By that time he had already produced several articles of literary criticism, including a very brief review of short stories by his friend, the Normandy writer Philippe de Chennevières. He had also published his witty pastiche of Balzac, 'How to pay your debts when you are a genius' which, however playful it might be, nevertheless indicates how deeply the young writer was steeped in the writings of the great novelist. And to these he had added the less than enthusiastic review of Louis Ménard's *Prométhée délivré*, which he had summarily dismissed as a philosophical poem, driven by 'the phantoms of reason' whereas true poetry is inspired by 'the phantoms of the imagination' (*oc*, II, p. 11). There was also the precocious 'Advice to Young Writers' which he published in 1846 and which began: 'The precepts you are about to read are the fruit of experience'. The deliberately ponderous opening, however, was immediately followed by the witty admission that 'experience implies a certain number of blunders'. This sparkling little tongue-in-cheek compendium of what to do and what to avoid covers such topics as salaries, how to pan someone else's work, methods of composition, inspiration ('inspiration is definitely the sister of daily work' (*oc*, ii, p. 18) remarks the poet who had such difficulty submitting to the discipline of daily work), mistresses and creditors. On this last topic Baudelaire sagaciously offers advice he himself consistently fails to follow: 'Never have any creditors; act as if you did have them if you must, but that's the most I'll allow' (*oc*, ii, p. 19).

At least two more critical articles were published before the study of 'honest' theatre. First there was a brief but careful review of short stories by Champfleury, the self-styled 'realist' writer with whom Baudelaire shared an enthusiasm for the popular theatre and, later, for the music of Richard Wagner. Second, in the summer of 1851, there appeared, as a preface to the songs of the so-called worker poet Pierre Dupont, Baudelaire's detailed introduction to the writer and his work. Like many of the great Romantics, Baudelaire claims in this preface to value most highly the poet who speaks for the people, and who remains constantly alert to contemporary human needs and concerns. The Dupont article can be read as a kind of template of Baudelaire's later criticism, with its desire to understand how the poet's early experiences formed the adult voice, its close attention to the central themes that create the atmosphere of the work, and its desire to move from the individual example to the broader context of art or literature. Moreover, he closes with a powerful poetic manifesto:

A great destiny lies before poetry! Happy or despondent, poetry always bears within it its divine and utopian nature. It constantly contradicts reality, for if it did not, it would cease to be. In the dungeon cell, poetry becomes revolt. At the hospital window, it is the ardent hope of health; in the dilapidated and dirty attic, poetry adorns itself like a fairy of luxury and elegance. Not only does poetry affirm, it also repairs. Everywhere poetry negates iniquity. (*oc*, ii, p. 35)

While Baudelaire's faith in the practical possibility of applying utopian dreams to social realities would sharply diminish in the years that followed Napoleon III's *coup d'état*, that sense of the relationship between revolt and poetry remained defiant and unshaken, however many dilapidated and dirty attics he inhabited.

Like the assessment of Dupont's works, the critique of the 'honest' plays and novels is, to a considerable extent, a literary manifesto, and it points forward to the masterly critical essays of Baudelaire's maturity. From the arresting opening sentence with its sardonic claim that 'a great rage of honesty has taken hold of the theatre and the novel' (*oc*, II, p. 38) to his caustic concluding judgement concerning the Montyon prize, which was given for the work of literature that best promoted the morality of the working class, this is a fiery argument for freeing literature from any demands of morality, and one that remains as compelling as it is timely. The school of good sense is contemptuously dismissed for its lowbrow promotion of petit-bourgeois values, but Baudelaire's prime purpose in this review is to explore what can legitimately be demanded of art. He concludes, in a judgement that projects a particularly clear light on his later writing: 'Vice is seductive and must be painted as seductive; but it brings in its wake exceptional moral illness and suffering, and these must be described' (*oc*, II, p. 42). This, indeed, is one of the central unspoken tenets in *Les Fleurs du mal*.

A couple of months later, he published a pendant piece, an attack on the so-called Pagan school of poets, who, he claimed, were constantly harking back to Greco-Roman antiquity and, unlike such writers as Pierre Dupont, were so out of touch with contemporary thinking that they 'would speak of the god Pan as they would of the prisoner of Saint Helena [Napoleon]' (*oc*, II, p. 44). The young critic who urged his contemporaries to attend to the wind of modernity argues forcefully in this article that 'to dismiss passion and reason is to kill literature'. If you deny the efforts of the society that has built your own, a society influenced by Christianity and by more recent philosophy, Baudelaire argues, you commit artistic suicide, because you thereby refuse the power and the means of achieving perfection, which stem from comprehending and responding to the contemporary. If you surround yourself exclusively with the seductions of art, you create massive chances of self-destruction, because, he contends, the 'springs that move the world will long remain hidden from you' (*oc*, II, p. 47). Neither extreme bourgeois virtue, locked in the here and now, nor extreme high art, incessantly harking back to classical antiquity, offer a solution: literature, Baudelaire affirms in his rousing conclusion, must 'rebuild its forces in a finer atmosphere. The time is not far off when it will be understood that any literature that refuses to walk fraternally between knowledge and philosophy is both homicidal and suicidal' (*oc*, II, p. 49). For once, Baudelaire strikes us as overly optimistic, but his optimism comes with an unmistakable edge of irony.

At the same time that Baudelaire was using the opportunity of literary criticism to position his own art, and in particular to affirm that beauty can never be pernicious, he was also forging ahead with his own creative writing, especially with poetry that focused on contemporary city life. In early 1852 he published, in *La Semaine théâtrale*, two poems that would later appear in the Parisian Pictures section of *Les Fleurs du mal*: 'Morning Twilight' and 'Evening Twilight'. In *La Semaine théâtrale*, the two poems follow a review by his friend Champfleury, who gallops idiosyncratically through various contemporary cultural events, including the painting of the realists Gustave Courbet and François Bonvin, concerts promoting the work of Beethoven, Haydn, Mozart, Weber and Mendelssohn and the publication of his own book, *Les Excentriques*. Most importantly he includes this defiant claim: 'There is a race of young, undisciplined writers, full of life and anger, who have something to try out, who are seeking a new architecture, solid and simple'.[3] It was Barbey d'Aurevilly who would suggest, in an article written in July 1857, that in *Les Fleurs du mal* Baudelaire had sought to organize his poems according to a secret architecture (*oc*, i, p. 798). At the least the reference to architecture in Champfleury's article suggests the importance and vibrancy of shared discussions, but may also indicate Baudelaire's role in influencing the vocabulary and the thinking of his friends.

The first of Baudelaire's two twilights swarms with a rich cast of the characters that will populate *Les Fleurs du mal*; prostitutes, the poor, the debauched and the dying, but it opens with the dreams of adolescents, as if to suggest the rapid progress from the dreams of the young to the reality of maturity and the end of life. The poem ends on a dour but powerful call to arms: trembling Dawn in her green and pink dress moves slowly along the deserted Seine, while that hardworking old man, sombre Paris, rubs his eyes and takes up his tools. The classical personification of Dawn as a rosy-fingered goddess is characteristically transformed into something at once more realistic and above all contemporary here by the poet who condemned the Pagan School. The counterpart poem, depicting evening twilight, is more sinister. The criminal welcomes evening's concealing darkness, while the poor, like scholars, can seek relief after a hard day's toil. But it is also the time when prostitution comes to life, when the city of mud opens up like a seething ants' nest. The poet tries to close his ears to all this uproar, but is filled with pity, which is also self-pity, for those who, because they have never known 'the sweetness of home', have 'never lived'. While neither poem is particularly experimental in terms of poetic technique, each draws on a wide vocabulary that brings together both high and low life, and each offers a powerful, unsentimental voice to those who have rarely been heard.

Two important stylistic influences converged in Baudelaire's thinking around this time, that of the conservative political philosopher, Joseph de Maistre, and the writing, both theoretical and creative, of the American, Edgar Allan Poe. In claiming that these two voices taught him to reason, Baudelaire, I would argue, is focusing less on content than on manner, paying tribute to the pithy compression of the first and to the carefully controlled focus of the second. By this time Baudelaire was already positioning himself beyond politics, quoting Vigny's claim that the poet's place was neither in a republic, nor in an absolute monarchy, nor in a constitutional monarchy, and noting with sardonic satisfaction that this was a claim that no one had been able refute (*oc*, II, pp. 250, 296).

In Poe, he would later maintain, he had found a brother, whose works included topics that Baudelaire himself had thought of, but that the American had carried out to perfection before him. His first study of Poe appeared in March and April 1852 in the *Revue de Paris*, an influential periodical belonging to Arsène Houssaye, who co-directed it with Maxime du Camp, Théophile Gautier and Louis de Cormenin, while the prolific Louis Ulbach acted as secretary. Baudelaire's article includes various revealing self-portraits, suggesting the extent to which the later criticism may also contain embedded and encrypted images of himself. Certainly the conclusion, with its proposed words for Poe's tombstone, reflect back on Baudelaire himself:

All you who have ardently striven to discover the laws of your being, who have aspired to the infinite, and whose unsatisfied feelings have been forced to seek horrible relief in the wine of debauchery, pray for him. Now that his purified corporeal being swims amid entities whose existence he glimpsed, pray for him who sees and who knows, and he will intercede for you. (*oc*, II, p. 288)

By this stage in his life Baudelaire was already deeply mired in that stark contrast between the real and the ideal, and seeking relief in a variety of what he would later term artificial paradises. In Poe, however, he found a figure who allowed him to discover a justification for that desire to look to external stimuli for the sources of personal artistic inspiration. It is undeniable, he would assert in his 1856 study on Poe, that intoxication makes it possible not only to link dreams together but also to create a form of reasoning that can be reproduced only by getting drunk again. 'I believe', Baudelaire adds, 'that in many cases, although certainly not in all of them, Poe's drunkenness was a form of mnemonics, a method of working, which was both energetic and fatal, but which was appropriate for his passionate nature. The poet learnt to drink just as a careful writer strengthens his skills by accumulating notebooks' (*oc*, ii, p. 315). If Baudelaire himself ever accumulated such notebooks, most of them must have been lost in the many moves he was forced to make in a Paris where he was dogged by creditors and where he would never know that 'sweetness of home' he longingly mentions in 'Evening Twilight'. There are various traces of such notes in his so-called intimate journals, passages where he sketches his view of the theatre, or of progress, but most of his notebooks are concerned less with strengthening writing or observational skills than with tightening moral and physical sinews.

That Baudelaire had been thinking for some time about the use of artificial aids in creating those mnemonic strategies he believed could help create great art is suggested both by his 1851 study, *On Wine and Hashish*, and by a poem he published in November 1854. The poem appeared in a periodical that rejoiced in the name *Jean Raisin, revue joyeuse et vinicole* (*John Grape, joyous and viticultural review*). 'The Rag-pickers' Wine' suggests an implicit comparison between the work of those who earn a precarious living by seeking out odd scraps of recyclable material and the practice of the poet, transforming the dross of the modern city into dreams of glory. The comparison had already appeared in *On Wine and Hashish*:

Here is a man whose task it is to collect the debris of the capital. Everything the great city has thrown away, everything it has lost, everything it has disdained, everything it has broken, he catalogues and collects. He consults the archives of debauchery and the clutter of refuse. He makes a selection, an intelligent choice. Like a miser gathering up treasure trove, he gathers garbage for the god of Industry to chew over and transform into objects of use or of pleasure . . . He stumbles over the paving stones, like young poets who spend their days wandering in search of rhymes. (*OC*, I, p. 381)

The poem would transform this into:

Often, in the street light's bright red fire,
The flame whipped by the wind as it rattles the cover,
In the heart of the old town, that labyrinth of mire,
Where humanity seethes in stormy disorder,

You see an old ragpicker nodding his head,
Tripping and bumping into walls like rhymesters,
And taking no notice of the spy, his subject,
He pours out his heart in glorious ventures. (*OC*, I, p. 106)

Baudelaire's somewhat perfidious friend, the photographer and cartoonist Nadar, has left us both a visual and a verbal caricature of the Baudelaire of these years. The cartoon, responding to the poem 'A Carcass', shows a fastidious Baudelaire, surrounded by spiky flowers, leaping back in disgust at the sight of a rotting corpse. In his verbal caricature, Nadar describes his friend in these terms:

Charles Baudelaire, a young poet who is touchy, bilious, irritable and irritating, and often completely disagreeable in private life. Very realistic despite his paradoxical behaviour, his literary form possesses all the style and severity of classical antiquity, and of those few spirits who walk these days in the solitude of

Félix Nadar,
*Caricature of
Baudelaire*, 1857,
charcoal drawing.

the *self*, I believe him to be the best and the surest of where he is
going. Very difficult to publish, moreover, because in his poems
he calls the good Lord an *imbecile*, Baudelaire has brought out
on the Salon of 1846 a book as remarkable as the best of
Diderot's articles.[4]

Baudelaire, himself a frequent caricaturist, sketched his own verbal
silhouette of Nadar, depicting him enviously as 'the most astonishing expression of vitality'. Reporting that Nadar's brother Adrien
claimed that Félix had a double quota of all his viscera, Baudelaire
adds, with a characteristic sting in the tail of his admiration: 'I
was envious to see him succeed so well in everything that is not
abstract' (*oc*, i, p. 695).

Baudelaire's prickliness and his refusal to write the kind of poetry that would guarantee him publication is also evident in his response to an invitation he received in 1853 from Fernand Desnoyers, an ambitious 25-year-old who believed himself to be one of his generation's greatest poets. Desnoyers wanted to publish an anthology of texts in homage to C. F. Denecourt, the enthusiastic nature-lover who had done so much to make the forest of Fontainebleau accessible to the general public. Baudelaire responded with a withering letter rejecting the conventional depiction of nature, but offering Desnoyers the two poems he had devoted to twilight, poems that are unashamedly urban:

> You ask me for some poetry for your little collection, poems on Nature, I believe? On woods, great oaks, greenery, insects – the sun, too, if I'm not mistaken? But you know very well that the vegetable kingdom fails to move me and that my soul rebels at that strange new religion that will always be, so it seems to me, rather *shocking* to any *spiritual* being. I'll never believe that the soul of the gods inhabits plants, and even if it could, I really couldn't work up much enthusiasm about it, and would consider my own soul as much more important than that of the sanctified vegetables. Moreover, I've always thought that *Nature*, flourishing, rejuvenated Nature, possessed something impudent and painful. (*c*, 1, p. 248)

A similar irritation with what is flourishing and rejuvenated also appears in his poem 'To one who is too cheerful', which dates from about this time, and was included in an unsigned letter to Apollonie Sabatier, his former neighbour on the Isle Saint-Louis. His scalding anger here bursts out in a series of furious denials of those who respond with undaunted happiness to the bleakness and decrepitude of the world. Reading this poem, we need to bear in mind that, like many of the poems that subsequently appeared in

Les Fleurs du mal, it has a counterpart, 'Confession', the poem in which the lovely and apparently imperturbable woman confesses the grinding toil involved in consistently presenting to the world that mask of happiness. The same theme would be taken up in Baudelaire's poem 'The Mask', a creative response to Ernest Christophe's statue of the same name, with its depiction of a woman who appears to be mindlessly simpering, whereas the smiling face is merely a mask concealing the real face, a face suffused with bitter tears.

Part of Baudelaire's irritability stems from the fact that the years immediately following the declaration of the Second Empire were increasingly difficult for him. His debts continued to accumulate, inflated by his habit of borrowing at high interest to pay creditors who were particularly pressing. This spiral of debt became progressively harder to break as the syphilis contracted in late adolescence reappeared, and he turned more and more to wine and opium, both to seek relief from his symptoms and in the hopes of heightening his artistic power. Two letters, each to his mother, one on 27 March 1852 and the other on 20 December 1855, offer a summary of his life to date and reflect on his relationship with Jeanne. In reading them, we should not forget that both his constant need for money and his complex relationship with Mme Aupick led to exaggerations that add a particularly lurid glow to his claims. Baudelaire writes the first letter in the noise and discomfort of a café, as he claims he is forced to write his articles in wine shops or reading rooms, and in a state of 'perpetual rage' (*c*, I, p. 192). The reason he gives for this need to work away from home is that 'Jeanne has become an obstacle not merely to [his] happiness . . . but also to the improvement of [his] mind' (*c*, I, p. 193). Writing, he claims, with tears of rage and shame in his eyes, he complains that it is impossible to exchange with Jeanne any conversation concerning politics or literature, that she would throw his manuscripts in the fire if by doing so she could get more money, that she does not admire him and makes his home a misery to him. He wants to leave her, but pride forbids him from doing so without giving her a large sum of money. And he also needs money to buy books, a deprivation adding further to his deep unhappiness. There is in this letter so transparent a desire to blackmail, so obvious a determination to work on his mother's sympathy in order to milk her for the highest possible sum, that it is easy to dismiss what is also obvious: that when he accuses Jeanne of not understanding and admiring him, the true target of this accusation is not her, but his mother, whom he believed incapable of seeing him as the great writer he knew himself to be.

Despite the three years between them, the letter of December 1855 deploys similar tactics: I have many things to tell you, I am suffering ('I am not positively old but will soon become so', writes the 34-year-old poet), 'I lack everything that might make my life moderately comfortable and above all I want to be admired as a poet'. The fear that he might die before he had written the body of work that would make his name runs powerfully through all this, although he knows this is the argument least likely to sway her:

> You are so completely unaware of what a poet's existence might be that no doubt you won't understand much of this argument, but that is the root of my main fear. I do not want to die in obscurity, I don't want to reach old age without having acquired a regular lifestyle, I'll NEVER resign myself to that, and I believe my person to be very precious, I'm not saying more precious than that of other people but sufficiently precious for me.
> (c, I, p. 327)

There is no mention of Jeanne in this letter, but he was to return to her yet again that very month, after a brief liaison with the actress Marie Daubrun, who had been Banville's mistress since 1852. Marie left Baudelaire to return to Banville, apparently causing no lasting ill-feeling between the two poets, who remained on friendly terms. Baudelaire would draw inspiration from Marie Daubrun's green eyes and her gentle affection to write his third cycle of love poems for *Les Fleurs du mal*, presenting her as the gentle but persistent lover who took what was left of the poet's ravaged heart, offering him the pleasures and sorrows of autumn's mists and waning suns.

Despite the physical conditions and practical difficulties he complained about to his mother, these were years that saw his translations of short stories by Poe, published first in periodicals in July 1854 and in April 1855. In 1856 came the publication of the first volume of Baudelaire's translations, *Histoires extraordinaires*,

Marie Daubrun, *c.* 1860, photograph by Etienne Carjat.

together with his lengthy introduction. Over the years he would use these introductions as a way of setting down a vision of the artist and an aesthetic code that reflected as much on him as on the American writer with whom he claimed to feel such sympathy. One thread that runs through the introductions is his thinking about ways in which the writer can defy the conditions of humdrum everyday existence and find a means of waking each morning with that intensity of feeling that makes colours stand out more brightly, sounds strike the ear with greater clarity and the mind function more sharply. As we have seen, Poe, according to Baudelaire, found a means of summoning up such moments through alcohol, for it was only when drunk that he could rediscover certain chains of thought and argument. This argument would be extended in the collection of essays known as *The Artificial Paradises*. But Poe's work also provided Baudelaire with an ideal vehicle to demonstrate the value he placed on what, inspired by Poe, he called the 'totality of effect' created by a work of literature. The gifted artist, he argues, in a revealing assertion, deliberately conceives of the effect to be produced and invents episodes, themes, and incidents most likely to achieve those ends. 'If the first sentence is not written with the aim of preparing the final impression', he asserts, 'the work has failed from the outset' (*oc*, ii, p. 329). Moreover, these studies on Poe allow him to intensify an argument adumbrated in earlier writing concerning the function of the different arts and their relationship with truth and morality. Poetry, he insists, cannot align itself to knowledge or morality, since poetry, instead of having truth as its object, has only itself. This does not mean that poetry cannot be moral, but it becomes so by focusing not on morality but instead on beauty, raising the reader's soul above the humdrum and banal and briefly revealing a more perfect universe.

It is at once by means of poetry and *through* poetry, by and *through* music, that the soul glimpses the splendours situated behind the tomb, and when an exquisite poem brings tears to our eyes, those tears are not the proof of an excess of pleasure, but rather bear witness to an upsurge of melancholy, of a postulation of the nerves, of a nature exiled in the imperfect and longing to seize hold immediately, on this very earth, of the paradise the poem has revealed. (*OC*, II, p. 334)

In parallel with his thinking about aesthetics, Baudelaire's long-term interest in caricature at last bore fruit with his publication in 1855 of 'On the Essence of Laughter', a philosophical study which he envisaged as introducing his essay on caricaturists. As he claims in his opening paragraph, this was a topic that had become a kind of obsession for him. We find the first reference to it on the back cover of his account of the 'Salon of 1845'. Then, in a letter to his mother of December 1847, he professes to have been working for the last eight months on two essays, one of which was a history of caricature. Two years later, Champfleury, drawing up a project for a review to be called *Le Hibou philosophe* (*The Philosopher Owl*), included in his list of titles 'On Caricature', by Baudelaire. A few weeks later, when Baudelaire sent the journalist Antoine Watripon his notes about his life and work, he included 'The Physiology of Laughter' as an article about to appear. While parts of the essay were indeed published in *L'Evénement* of 20 April 1851, it was not until 1855 that an abbreviated form of it would appear, and then only in an obscure journal called *Le Portefeuille*. In 1857 his essay on caricaturists came out in *Le Présent*, to be republished the following year in a much more prestigious review, *L'Artiste*. The study on laughter itself, however, did not reach the attention of the broader public until after Baudelaire's death, when it was published by Michel Lévy as part of Baudelaire's art criticism. If the publication took so long to come about, it was not that Baudelaire's interest in it was flagging or that he felt displeased with it. On the contrary, this is a highly ambitious and original essay, and Baudelaire's reluctance to publish it in leading periodicals before it had been honed and polished to his satisfaction is proof of his awareness of what he had achieved. As Claude Pichois argues (*oc*, ɪɪ, p. 1344), it is typical of him that he allowed a section, that on Pierrot, to be published separately, as a kind of trial to test the waters before he released the complete essay. As we shall see, he would do something analogous with *Les Fleurs du mal*.

The comic, Baudelaire argues in this essay, is 'a monstrous phenomenon' (*oc*, ɪɪ, p. 530), intimately linked with 'an ancient fall, a physical and moral degradation' (*oc*, ɪɪ, p. 528). We laugh only because we feel superior to the person or situation that arouses our laughter. Baudelaire divides the comic into an absolute form, such as the grotesque, and a comic of meaning, which has two elements, one artistic and one moral. This division allows him to introduce further categories, primarily contrasting different nations, but above all it allows him to insist on the duality both of art, which carries with it an eternal and a fleeting component, and of the artist, who can be an artist only by being double and knowing every aspect of that dual nature. This theme of the *homo duplex* runs through much of Baudelaire's writing, receiving a particularly powerful expression here and in the two studies of caricature, one devoted to French artists and the other to foreign caricaturists.

These are remarkable studies, not only in their breadth of coverage but also in the way in which Baudelaire, while offering close analyses of the artists and their works, also sets them in a particular national and chronological context. Brueghel, he notes in passing, created his splendid menagerie of monsters at the time of the 'epidemic of witches' (*oc*, ɪɪ, p. 574), while Goya not only typifies Spanish gaiety, joviality and satire as in the good old days of Cervantes but also, more profoundly, succeeds in creating realistic monsters and in so doing pushes the boundaries of creative art further than any other painter. Small wonder, given the density and originality of these explorations of laughter both in general and in the way it can be captured in the visual arts, that Baudelaire, although eager to see them in print and desperate for the money they might bring in, held these essays back until he felt they were ready to be published.

If 1855 saw the first publication, however fragmentary, of his theory of laughter, it was also important for another event. In the first half of the nineteenth century, the French had established themselves as leaders in industrial exhibitions, but they were abruptly upstaged by the British, who hosted a spectacular international exhibition in 1851, housed in the remarkable Crystal Palace. Napoleon III's pride demanded some kind of response and in 1855, against the grim background of the Crimean War, the French capital mounted what was described as a world exhibition. It proved to be a financial failure but a popular success for Napoleon III and it furnished the occasion for a visit to Paris by Queen Victoria and Prince Albert, the first time the reigning British monarchy had come to France since Henry V, 400 years earlier.

The exhibition gave Baudelaire a further opportunity to establish himself as an art critic and more importantly still to argue against narrow-minded aesthetic judgements. His analysis, indeed, opened with a statement of his critical method that shows how far he had moved since the Salons of 1845 and 1846, how much he is now interested in comparisons across countries, not in any desire to establish a hierarchy but rather to emphasize their equal role in creating what he terms 'the harmony of the universe'. The critic, he insists, should be above all 'a dreamer whose mind is turned both to generalization and to the study of details' (oc, II, p. 575). Only such a dreamer, he implies, can respond adequately to the beauties revealed by, for instance, the Chinese pavilion, which most critics in fact completely ignored, with the exception of Théophile Gautier, who saw in it only examples of grotesque ugliness. How, Baudelaire asks, can we learn to see the beauty of products whose aesthetic codes are completely unknown to us? His answer is significant, in light of his own creative writing as well as for what it reveals about his refusal to be bound by conventions and prejudices. We need, he tells us, to transform ourselves by a phenomenon of will acting on the imagination, in order to be able to step into the milieu that has given birth to this 'strange flowering' as he puts it (*oc*, II, p. 576). He acknowledges that few people possess this wonderful gift of cosmopolitanism, but suggests that we can all acquire it by setting preconceptions aside and letting ourselves be penetrated by new and different forms of beauty. Systems don't help, however tempting they may appear, for the simple and powerful reason that beauty, being always bizarre, cannot be locked into a system (*oc*, II, p. 577–8). Cosmopolitanism is an important concept in Baudelaire's thinking, a value he placed high on the scale. Gautier, for example, is depicted as possessing a mind that is 'a cosmopolitan mirror of beauty' (*oc*, II, p. 108), allowing him to 'know, love and explain' Asiatic, Greek, Roman, Spanish, Flemish, Dutch and English beauty (*oc*, II, p. 123). The artist Constantin Guys also possesses this particular virtue, and in his 'Salon of 1846' Baudelaire had depicted himself as an enthusiastic traveller, a 'cosmopolitan spirit who prefers beauty to glory' (*oc*, II, p. 470).

The bizarreness of beauty, like the need to keep an open, cosmopolitan mind when exploring works of art, was not just a theoretical aesthetic tenet for Baudelaire. Both were about to become central to his very existence as a poet as he began to prepare his poems for publication not just separately but as a whole. Ever cautious in this regard, he made a trial run in 1855 by publishing a group of eighteen under the collective title 'Les Fleurs du mal', a title invented earlier that year by the critic Hippolyte Babou, whose *Lettres satiriques et critiques* Poulet-Malassis would publish in 1860. Nadar has left us a photograph of Babou. Looking like a somewhat podgy dandy, with his cravat carefully tied and his hair neatly curled, he seems an unlikely source for that oxymoronic title.

However cautious he may have been about publishing his poems, Baudelaire was no diplomat when it came to dealing with the editorial boards of reviews. The letter he sent in April 1855 to Victor De Mars, the secretary of the prestigious *Revue des deux mondes*, is characteristic in its refusal to bear in mind the needs of an audience, either the letter's immediate recipient or that of the journal itself:

> I am preparing a very fine *Epilogue* for *Les Fleurs du mal* and hope to complete it in time. I wanted to tell you this – that I am very eager that whatever poems you choose you should let me put them in order *with you*, in such a way that they create, so to speak, a suite, – just as we did for the first group . . .
>
> The Epilogue (addressed to a lady) says more or less this: *Let me rest in your love. – But no, – love will give me no rest. – Frankness and kindness are repulsive. – If you wish to please me and rekindle our desire, be cruel, be a liar and a libertine, be vile and a thief; – and if you're not willing to be all that, I'll thrash you, without anger. For I am irony's true agent and my illness is of a kind that is absolutely beyond cure.* – That, as you see, makes a pretty firework display of monstrosities, *a real Epilogue*, worthy of the *prologue* to the reader, a real Conclusion. (*c*, I, p. 312)

Hardly likely to reassure or endear an editor, this sardonic claim does at least indicate both that Baudelaire was already preoccupied with the order of his poems, if not yet as much as he would become for the second edition, and that he was outspokenly determined to overthrow conventional images of love, beauty and poetry itself. It seems that Baudelaire did not complete this epilogue, although traces of it can be found in his poem 'L'Héautontimorouménos' (The Self-torturer), which he first wrote out in an album in 1855. The eighteen poems that appeared concluded with 'Love and the Skull' which could be seen as an equally bleak if less openly provocative commentary on love, with cupid squatting on a skull and blowing bubbles made of human brains, blood and flesh.

The poem used to open this group was 'To the Reader', suggesting that whether or not Baudelaire saw it as a prelude, the subtitle given it by Gautier and Banville after his death, this poem did represent a worthy opener. There is however a text that intervenes between the title *Les Fleurs du mal* and the poem, in the form of a footnote, probably written by Emile Montégut, soon to become the journal's main literary critic and already familiar to its readers through his criticism and through his translations from Emerson and Macauley (he would later translate the complete works of Shakespeare). The note both justifies the poems' inclusion in the journal and acts itself as a 'to the reader' clarifying editorial policy:

> In publishing the lines you are about to read, we believe we are revealing that yet again the spirit that animates us is favourable to all kinds of experiments and tryouts. What we believe deserving of interest here is the lively, curious expression, however violent, of certain failings, certain moral afflictions of which, without sharing or discussing them, one needs to be aware as signs of our times. We consider moreover that there are cases where publicity is not merely an encouragement, but where it can have the influence of a useful word of advice, and summon true talent to free itself, to strengthen itself, by extending its pathways and broadening its horizons.[5]

A touch nervous, a little paternalistic in suggesting that by publishing some of his poems the journal might help the poet spread his wings, trying a little too hard to reveal an open mind, and tucked away in the middle that claim that we not only don't share these weaknesses but we don't normally so much as talk about them, even if we realize that if we are to be aware of our times we need to have some intellectual familiarity with them. In other words, a no doubt well-meaning but nonetheless complete failure to respond to the main challenge of 'To the Reader', in which, precisely, we are urged to acknowledge ourselves as the poet's hypocrite siblings. In addition to the review's footnote, there is an epigraph, subsequently excised from the final version, although it still appears in the 1857 edition, where it is quoted on the cover: six lines from the seventeenth-century poet Théodore Agrippa d'Aubigné:

> They say you must pour all things that are vile
> In the coffin's locked hold, in oblivion's phial,
> And that writing restores the power of iniquity
> To contaminate the morals of all our posterity,
> But wickedness has never been science's spawn
> And virtue has never of ignorance been born.

The journal's claim is being backed here by a very similar contention more powerfully put: it's not knowledge that breeds vice, just as virtue does not spring from ignorance. Pouring horrible things down the sink, like sweeping them under the carpet, merely results in smelly sinks and lumpy carpets. Somewhere between this publication and that of the second edition Baudelaire abandoned the epigraph, perhaps reluctant to let other voices speak for his poetry, a reluctance that would be mirrored by his unwillingness and indeed inability to write a preface to his volume of poetry.

In addition to 'To the Reader' and the closing poem 'Love and the Skull' this grouping of poems contained enough to astonish readers of the *Revue des deux mondes*, in terms both of the themes explored and of the poetic technique deployed. 'Reversibility' contrasted an angelic woman characterized by gaiety, goodness, health, beauty and happiness, with the anger, hatred, fevers and age of her poet-lover, but concluded that whereas the biblical King David might have begged her, on his deathbed, to give him the health of her lovely body, all the poet would request was her prayers. This poem's ironic counterpart, 'Confession', in which the woman confides in her companion just what hard work it is to keep up appearances of beauty and serenity, was also part of the group, not immediately following 'Reversibility' as it does in the second edition of *Les Fleurs du mal*, but separated from it only by the sonnet titled 'The Cask of Hate' in which the classical image of the daughters of Danaus, punished for the murders of their bridegrooms by being condemned eternally to gather water in eternally leaking pots, is transformed into an image of hatred, endlessly unsatisfied by acts of brutal and bloody vengeance.

Next in the group was another sonnet, 'The Spiritual Dawn', which like 'Reversibility' and 'Confession' became part of a cycle of poems evoking a more spiritual love, poems that Baudelaire sent anonymously to Madame Sabatier, claiming that they were inspired by her. Here again the woman is called on to provide a guiding light to the debauched but idealistic lover, struck low, but still dreaming and still suffering. On the smouldering debris of stupid orgies, he tells her, your memory, brighter, rosier, more charming, floats ceaselessly before my eyes. 'Destruction', which followed in the *Revue des deux mondes* grouping, provides a bitter contrast with 'Spiritual Dawn' for here the poet is accompanied not by the benevolent guiding goddess of love, but by the Devil:

The Devil is constantly stirring beside me,
Swimming around me like impalpable air.
I swallow him and feel him burning my lungs
Filling my heart with the longing for evil.

Knowing of course my great love for the arts,
He sometimes appears as the loveliest woman,
And under fictitious pretences of boredom
Accustoms my lips to infamous potions,

Thus leading me far from the eyes of the Lord.
Gasping and broken with weariness I wander
The great plains of Boredom, extensive and empty,

And he hurls in my eyes that are full of confusion
Filth-stained apparel and wide-open wounds,
All of Destruction's foul bloodstained tool kit. (*OC*, I, p. 111)

The power of the poem, the intensity and physicality of its images, and the telling rhymes that in the French link art with boredom and woman with infamy, must have struck the readers of the journal, even if the violence and brutality of this poem surely make it one of those that the editors felt most anxious about publishing. Another poem destined to find its place in the section of *Les Fleurs du mal* that focuses on debauchery and destruction, the section that bears the title 'Fleurs du Mal', followed 'Destruction' in the review: 'A Voyage to Cythera'. Here the pretty images chosen by French Rococo artists when they depicted the island of Venus are thrown brutally aside to make way for a nightmare vision in which the traditional doves are replaced by ferocious birds feeding on a body hanging from a gibbet, a body moreover in which the poet recognizes his own decaying image. Give me the strength and courage, he concludes, to contemplate my heart and body without disgust. Only in this way, the poem implies, will he reach a poetic truth about both love and physical existence that will raise his poetry above the level of the conventional.

The Latin title of the next poem in the group, '*Moesta et errabunda*' blends ideas of sadness with a longing to wander, whether applied to a woman or to songs is not clear. Using the five-line stanza he often favours and that brings the first line back at the end of the verse to intensify a question or to add nostalgia for something lost in the past, something that can be recalled only by such rhetorical stratagems, the poem includes several of the themes that will dominate *Les Fleurs du mal*: the longing for a purity unobtainable in the foul modern city; the consolation provided by the sea; nostalgia for the scented paradise of childhood innocence; the erotic nature of that innocent period of life.

With 'The Split Bell' the attention turns to the poet himself, the quatrains of the sonnet evoking the bittersweet winter evenings when, sitting by the fire, you listen to the bells ringing out in the mists and fogs. The poet, however, is like a bell that has split, so that when he seeks to fill the air with his songs, all that he can produce is a muffled cry, like the death rattle of a wounded man dying alone on a battlefield. Similarly, 'The Enemy' laments the loss of youth and vigour, grieving that time may devour his life before he has been able to produce the new flowers of which he dreams.

By contrast 'A Former Life' seems closer to the poems written by such poets as Gautier and Leconte de Lisle after the disillusionment of the *coup d'état*, when they turned to art for art's sake. Its rich rhymes and its lush images, drawing on the sights and sounds of exotic sunsets at sea, as well as its static vision of calm pleasures, seem to hark back more to a lost paradise already vitiated by a 'painful secret' than to listen to the winds of modernity that Baudelaire had urged on the attention of his contemporaries in his review of the 1846 Salon. It is sharply different from the next poem in the grouping, '*De profundis clamavi*', a poem marked by images of polar landscapes and endless night, and with the virulent late romantic imagery of 'Posthumous Remorse' which seeks revenge on the poet's beautiful dark mistress by imagining her in the tomb, punished for her cruelty by what Poe had termed 'the conqueror worm'. The next in the sequence, 'Bad Luck', is, as Baudelaire would himself admit at a later date, little more than an unacknowledged translation of Henry Wadsworth Longfellow ('Art is long and time is fleeting / And our hearts, though stout and brave/ Still, like muffled drums are beating / Funeral marches to the grave') and Thomas Gray ('Full many a flower is born to blush unseen / And waste its sweetness on the desert air') while 'The Vampire' takes us back to the atmosphere of 'Posthumous Remorse' with its violent depiction of a powerful and destructive sexual attraction.

While Baudelaire may have urged Victor de Mars to work with him to create a 'suite' of poems, there is in this grouping little hint as yet of that desire for a secret architecture that can be detected in the first edition of *Les Fleurs du mal* and would be even stronger when he published the second edition. Nevertheless, through the power and intensity of his images and themes, as well as through the range of his prosodic structures, the variety he introduced into his sonnets and the suggestive power of his rhymes, he must have left a profound mark on readers willing to approach the poems with an acceptance of beauty in all its bizarreness.

An undated photograph Nadar took of him at around this time shows a somewhat wary Baudelaire, caught in movement, his high forehead revealed by increasing baldness, his cravat raffishly tied, his hands in his pockets, and his eyes blazing with the irascible intelligence that marks much of his writing from these years. A more formal photograph focuses attention on the determined, rather thin-lipped mouth, the dome of the forehead, the judgemental gaze of the dark eyes. What Baudelaire emphasizes when he sketches himself at this period are a slightly down-turned mouth, with deep lines around it, a long, uptilted nose, the balding forehead and that wary gaze. And almost always there is the extravagantly tied cravat, which seems almost to have a life of its own.

In 1857 he began to prepare his poems for publication in book form. He initially planned to include a resounding dedication to his 'master and friend' Théophile Gautier in which he referred to the poems as a 'dictionary of melancholy and crime' (*oc*, I, p. 187), apparently completely unaware, or careless, of what effect that expression might have on readers. For once he followed advice and toned the dedication down, so that it now reads: 'to the impeccable poet, the perfect magician of French Literature, my very dear and

Félix Nadar, *Charles Baudelaire, c.* 1855.

Félix Nadar, *Charles Baudelaire, c.* 1855.

greatly venerated master and friend Théophile Gautier, with the feelings of deepest humility I dedicate these sickly flowers'. After months spent correcting proofs and worrying about such matters as typeface and uniform spaces between the lines, Baudelaire had the pleasure of seeing *Les Fleurs du mal* published, by his friend Poulet-Malassis, on 28 June 1857. It was a handsome little volume, with the words 'Fleurs du mal' picked out in red, as were the publisher's logo and the name 'Poulet-Malassis et de Broise' (the latter being Poulet-Malassis's brother-in-law and reluctant business partner). The typeface is elegant, on the small side, and surrounded by much white space. In addition to 'To the Reader' the book is divided into five sections, 'Spleen and Ideal', 'Flowers of Evil', 'Revolt', 'Wine' and 'Death'. The volume closes on 'The Death of Artists', the hundredth poem (Baudelaire does not include 'To the Reader' in the numbered sequence). A hundred poems: Dante's *Divine*

Comedy has one hundred cantos in total, but whereas Dante's work leads his poet to paradise, the first edition of *Les Fleurs du mal* closes on an entirely secular note, with the artists hoping only that death, 'hovering like a new sun', will at long last make the flowers of their brains blossom.

The timing was not good. In late January and early February Gustave Flaubert had been taken to court, accused of immorality in his novel *Madame Bovary*, which had been serialized in the *Revue de Paris* the year before. Probably the real reason for this trial was political: the Second Empire, with a prudent eye to its conservative supporters, professed an intransigent morality which led to the trials of many writers and publishers whose depictions of a more realistic morality put them at odds with the government. Flaubert was exonerated and no doubt this failure to convict him sharpened government resolve to impose its views at the next possible opportunity. It certainly embittered the prosecuting attorney, Ernest Pinard, and made him all the more determined not to be vanquished when that opportunity came. But it might not have been Baudelaire who provided the next opportunity had it not been for a scathing review, which appeared on 5 July in *Le Figaro* and in which the poet was accused of producing 'monstrosities'. 'The odious rubs shoulders with the ignoble', wrote the critic, adding for good measure: 'the repulsive blends with the nauseating'. He specifically mentioned the poems entitled 'Denial', 'Lesbos' and 'Damned Women'. The last two poems evoke lesbian love, while the first, inspired by Saint Peter's denial of Christ, depicts God as a tyrant gorged with meat and wine, intoxicated by the symphony created by the sobbing of the martyred and the tortured. The poem concludes that St Peter had done well to deny all knowledge of Christ. Of these three, only 'Lesbos' was among the poems ordered to be removed from the volume, but the damage had been done, and once official attention had turned to the book, matters moved swiftly.

By 7 July 1857 even the insouciant Baudelaire realized that there was a very strong possibility that he and Poulet-Malassis would be prosecuted, and he began to prepare a supporting dossier. On 11 July he sent his publisher an excited letter:

> Quick! Hide, and I mean *hide carefully* the entire edition; you should have 900 unbound copies. There were still one hundred at Lanier's [the printers]. The men there seemed very surprised that I should wish to save 50 of them. I have put them in a safe place and signed a receipt. So there are 50 to feed the Cerberus of Justice. (*c*, I, p. 412)

The tone is one more of excited pleasure than exasperation or anxiety. At this early stage Baudelaire strikes us as being more pleasurably stimulated by the sense of having stirred up a hornets' nest than afraid of any destructive consequences. Indeed, through most of the subsequent trial he seems to have been convinced not only that he would be completely exonerated, but that he would benefit from the increased publicity the court proceedings brought him. He even announced to his, admittedly naive, friend Asselineau that he had been sure that the court would publicly restore his honour to him. Nevertheless, he set about collecting notes for his lawyer, Gustave Chaix d'Est-Ange, and trying to whip up support among the very few friends he had who might exert any influence. Whereas Flaubert had been able to call on many friends with power and influence in the Second Empire's governing spheres and was, moreover, strongly supported by his family, Baudelaire's bohemian lifestyle meant that he had few such powerful friends, and he had no family support. His mother had been recently widowed by the death of Aupick on 28 April 1857 and was in no position to help him. There was, however, at least one powerful political voice he hoped would speak in his favour: that of Prosper Mérimée, who, in addition to being a gifted short-story writer, had been appointed a senator for life in 1853. Sainte-Beuve, on whom he had confidently counted, pussy-footed around, unwilling to do much for a writer he never seems to have valued particularly highly. The writer Jules Barbey d'Aurevilly, however, wrote a perceptive and powerfully expressed article on his behalf as well as nudging him to prepare his case, something Baudelaire seems to have been reluctant to do.

He was also anxious to have a woman speak up for him, as Flaubert had had the support of the princess Mathilde. He eventually, but belatedly, decided on Madame Sabatier, who did what she could, which was very little in the time available to her. Realizing that she could not do much to change the verdict, Mme Sabatier seems to have decided to offer him the sole reward that was truly in her power: herself. At some point between 18 August and the end of the month, there was a brief, intense affair, which, while it clearly was not the fiasco some of the poet's more malicious acquaintances proclaimed it, repelled him by its revelation of the profoundly physical qualities of a woman he had elevated to sainthood.

On 20 August Baudelaire was summoned to appear in court. His lawyer, Chaix d'Est-Ange, did little to support his client, using little other than the latter's notes in response to the accusations made by Pinard, the prosecuting lawyer. The main defence offered was that the great poets who had preceded him had taken all the poetic themes save that of evil and suffering, and that in any case the morality of art lies in its beauty and not in its subject matter. Moreover, if Baudelaire were to be condemned, what great writer could not be held equally guilty?

These arguments proved unconvincing, and Baudelaire was condemned to pay a fine of 300 francs, together with the suppression from the volume of 'The Jewels', 'Lethe', 'To One Who Is Too Cheerful', 'In the Bright Light of Languishing Lamps', 'Lesbos' and 'The Metamorphoses of the Vampire', which were all seen as offending public morality. A pen drawing by the poet himself

Baudelaire, *Cartoon Self-portrait*, *c.* 1857–8, pen and ink, crayon and wash.

shows him gazing avidly at a bag labelled 10,000,000, apparently full of gold coins but possessed of wings that are bearing it rapidly away. On the left of the same sheet of paper is Champfleury and lower down, on the right, is another view of Baudelaire, this time saying to Gautier, 'not a penny'.

Enraged by the court's decision, and forced as a result to reconsider and rework his volume, he was to transform it into something far richer and far more complex, building into it a stronger structure and bringing the total number of poems to 126. The court had in fact done Baudelaire a curious and significant service, whipping him into a creative fervour that would produce some of his finest writing, both critical and creative.

4

The Results of the Trial

A letter written at the end of December 1857 suggests that Baudelaire
is one of those who, as he says in his 'Hashish Poem', 'know how to
observe themselves and retain the memory of their impressions, one
of those who, like [the German writer] Hoffmann, have succeeded
in constructing their own spiritual barometer' (*oc*, I, p. 401). In that
letter an apparently desolate and weary, but typically introspective
and self-analytical Baudelaire described his mood to his mother,
now quietly ensconced at the seaport of Honfleur, in a little house
that Aupick had bought some years earlier as a holiday home:

> Certainly, I have much to complain about in myself, and I'm
> utterly astonished and alarmed at the state I find myself in. Do I
> need a move? I don't know. Is it the physical malady diminishing
> mind and will, or spiritual cowardice wearying the body? I don't
> know. But what I feel is an immense despondency, a feeling of
> unbearable isolation, a perpetual fear of some vague misfortune,
> a total loss of faith in my strength, a complete absence of longing,
> an inability to find any kind of amusement. The bizarre success
> of my book and the hatred it has aroused interested me for a
> short while and then after that I fell back into the same state. You
> see, my dear mother, that I'm in a fairly serious state of mind for
> a man whose profession is to produce and adorn fictions. I keep
> asking myself: what's the point of this? What's the point of that?
> This truly is the state of spleen. (*c*, I, pp. 437–8)

Although he described himself as sunk deep in spleen, a depiction that seems confirmed by Carjat's photograph of him, in which he glares at us across the intervening decades, Baudelaire was entering upon the most productive period of his life. Above all, it was a time when, as the critic Richard D. E. Burton argues in a study entirely devoted to the poet's production in 1859, Baudelaire would for once be happy.[1] Part of that happiness stemmed from his mother's unexpectedly warm response to *Les Fleurs du mal*. A manuscript recently sold at auction, a letter dated 7 May 1858 and written to his half-brother Alphonse, reveals a degree of enthusiasm that may well surprise those who see Mme Aupick as consistently condemning her younger son. *Les Fleurs du mal*, she writes, contains moments of great beauty. 'There are certain stanzas that are admirable, revealing a purity of language, a simplicity of form that produce one of the most magnificent poetical effects. He possesses to an eminent degree the art of writing.' And she adds that his translations of Edgar Poe are 'very remarkable, even astonishing, equivalent to an original work of art.'[2] It was a period marked by the oscillation between pleasant dreams of moving permanently to Honfleur to live with his mother in her house looking over the estuary, and a heightened awareness of the specific stimulus he, and with him modern writers and painters, drew from the big city.

The continuing political instability of Paris, despite Haussmann's physical changes, was brought vividly home to its inhabitants on the evening of 14 January 1858 when a bomb thrown by the Italian republican Felice Orsini killed eight people and wounded a further 142 but narrowly failed to assassinate Napoleon III, who, ironically enough, was on his way to attend Rossini's opera about the revolutionary William Tell. Orsini had misguidedly hoped that the assassination would provoke an uprising in France that would inspire a similar movement in Italy. The French government seized the pretext to suppress many of the liberal periodicals in which Baudelaire had been able to place his writing. Partly as a response to

Etienne Carjat, *Charles Baudelaire, c.* 1860.

this state of affairs and partly no doubt out of sheer desperation with his financial situation, on 12 October 1858 Baudelaire signed a contract with the publisher Alphonse de Calonne in which he promised to provide 180 printed pages per year in exchange for 3,000 francs. This was a desperate measure for the constantly procrastinating poet, but one in which there entered a certain feeling of vengeance, since it was in Calonne's periodical that the fatal article denouncing

Les Fleurs du mal had appeared, and extracting money from the editor seemed some kind of recompense. As early as the beginning of the year, moreover, Baudelaire had drawn up a list of articles that he could write for Calonne, including a study of hashish, an analysis of those painters who 'subordinate art to reasoning' (the never-completed 'Philosophical Art' of which he left only a few pages of dense and suggestive notes), a close analysis of Poe's *Eureka* and a study of museums that have disappeared, or that should be created, a suggestion qualified by the annotation 'Spanish museum, English museum, etc.' (*c*, I, p. 449). The fact that he never completed this last article is one of the most regrettable of all perhaps for admirers of his art criticism. An earlier list, sent to his mother in July 1857, included his collected articles on art, under the title *Aesthetic Curiosities*, his adaptation of De Quincey's confessions, and a group referred to as *Nocturnal Poems*, a selection of prose poems that appeared in *Le Présent* on 24 August 1857.

Indeed, it is typical of Baudelaire that despite the mood of deep depression he had described to his mother at the end of 1857, he was still brimming with plans and projects. In a letter he wrote her in mid-February 1858, he claimed:

> I have in my head twenty novels and two plays. I don't want an honest and commonplace reputation; I want to crush people's minds, astonish them, like Byron, Balzac and Chateaubriand. My God, is there still time? – Oh, if only I'd known the value of time and health and money when I was a young man! (*c*, I, p. 451)

Astonish, *étonner*: this is a vital word in Baudelaire's vocabulary. It's the word he chooses to translate 'wonder' in Poe's expression, 'it is a happiness to wonder' (*oc*, II, p. 616). He proclaims that 'the unexpected, the surprising, the astonishing' is an 'essential and characteristic aspect of beauty' (*oc*, I, p. 656). And on several

Johan Barthold Jongkind, *Honfleur*, 1865, oil on canvas.

occasions he insists that Beauty is always astonishing. It is significant, therefore, that when he wrote to Poulet-Malassis describing his mother's house at Honfleur, the toy house as he termed it affectionately, he should argue that perched above the sea as it was, with a garden that provided the perfect ornamentation to set it off, it was 'made to astonish the eyes' (*c*, I, p. 521). Johan Barthold Jongkind's painting of 1865 gives us some idea of what Baudelaire found so attractive about the town and its setting. For months he would plan to move there permanently and immerse himself in quiet reading and writing, free from the destructive distractions of Paris. Several of his poems are imbued with the colours, sounds and atmosphere of that maritime landscape. But however serious they may have been, such dreams proved abortive. A brief visit starting in January 1859 served to make him aware of just how difficult those dreams would be to realize. First there was the problem of finding a source for the daily doses of opium in the form of laudanum that he now needed to alleviate the intestinal pain he suffered as a result of syphilis. In addition he recognized how much he needed the creative stimulus of Paris, whose rapidly changing face and seething

Edouard Manet, *Jeanne Duval Reclining*, 1862, oil on canvas.

crowds were inspiring some of his most powerful poems. And, finally, he had underestimated how guilty he would feel in abandoning the now chronically ill Jeanne. Manet's portrait of her, made in 1862, shows her surrounded and imprisoned in a voluminous skirt that fills the foreground and against which her legs seem disproportionately small, perhaps suggesting the paralysis that was afflicting her by this time. She carries something that at first looks like a book but that on closer inspection proves to be a fan. It is a disturbing portrait, one in which the personality of the sitter is almost completely absorbed into the shades and textures of her clothing. Looking at this canvas, it is difficult not to feel that Manet is expressing much of the complexity of his friend's relationship with her at the time when the love affair had degenerated into something far blacker, a responsibility and a torment.

Clearly it was only in Paris that Baudelaire could find the creative stimulus that is perhaps at its most obvious in the poems he wrote in the years between the two editions of *Les Fleurs du mal*. Spurred on by what he referred to as the humiliation of the trial, he was determined not merely to replace the six poems the Tribunal had excised, but to add something closer to twenty, transforming the volume into a work that, as he belligerently asserted to Calonne, would ensure he was understood, so that only those acting in complete bad faith could fail to see the 'voluntary impersonality' of his poems (c, I, p. 523). Among these additions are some of his most beautiful, most experimental and most famous verse poems.

Some of that creative vigour is reflected, moreover, in a letter written to his friend Asselineau in February 1859. In a letter that crackles with an energy that is all too rare in his correspondence, Baudelaire asks whether 'Macabre Dance', his poem inspired by a statue created by the sculptor Ernest Christophe, has appeared; urges Asselineau to 'insinuate' that the article on Théophile Gautier,

Félix Nadar,
Charles Asselineau,
?1850s.

Charles Meryon, *View of Notre-Dame across the Seine*, 1855, etching.

written with 'demonic rapidity', appear in its entirety and not be
divided up among several numbers of *L'Artiste* (it was published as
a whole on March 13 of that year); and begs him to 'pilfer' (*carotter*)
from Edouard Houssaye all Charles Meryon's views of Paris that he
can lay hands on. As Baudelaire's account of the Salon of 1859 would
reveal, Meryon had aroused Baudelaire's admiration for his represen-
tations of Paris, hauntingly beautiful etchings of cityscapes, often
populated by strange figures reminiscent of the work of the fifteenth-
century Dutch painter Hieronymus Bosch. Baudelaire goes on to
promise that, in the first days of March, he would arrive in Paris
with a 'monstrous packet' for Jean Morel, the director of the *Revue
française*. This would include his translation of Poe's poem 'The
Raven', together with Poe's 'famous commentary,' 'The Philosophy
of Composition' (Morel would publish this on 20 April 1859), and
some 'nocturnal poems', the generic term he used at this point for
his prose poems.

Baudelaire's preamble to his translation of 'The Philosophy of
Composition' is worth quoting at this point because, as so often in
writing about someone he admires, Baudelaire is also sketching an
idealized portrait of himself. Of course Poe had a great genius and
abundant inspiration, he argues, but he also loved work more than

anyone else did: 'he would often repeat, he who was a complete original, that originality is a matter of apprenticeship, which is not the same as something that can be conveyed by teaching . . . It will always be useful to reveal what benefits can be drawn from reflection and to show society people the amount of work that goes into creating that luxury item called Poetry' (*oc*, II, p. 344). Baudelaire's reputation as an inspired translator of Poe is based largely on his versions of the tales. Not wanting to lose the pleasure of rhythm and rhyme, he normally rejected any temptation to translate Poe's poetry, but in order to justify the arguments of the 'Philosophy of Composition' he was compelled to offer a French version of 'The Raven', to which, Poe claimed, perhaps tongue in cheek, that he had applied the precepts he sets out there. Forcing poetry into the mould of prose for his translation, Baudelaire admits, involves an 'immense imperfection', but one that is less bad than the 'monkey business' (*singerie*) of producing a translation in rhyme. To alleviate that imperfection as far as he could, Baudelaire offers a way of reading that also sheds light on the energetic attention he expects readers to pay to works of literature:

Use your memory to hear the most plaintive stanzas of Lamartine, the most magnificent and complex rhythms of Victor Hugo; combine with those memories that of the most subtle and wide-ranging tercets of Théophile Gautier – those from *Ténèbres* for example, that chaplet of formidable conceits on death and noth-ingness where the three-part rhyme fits so well with the obsessive melancholy – and you may perhaps obtain an approximate idea of Poe's talents as a versifier. I say versifier because it is I believe superfluous to speak of his imagination. (*oc*, II, p. 344)

The importance of memory, the ways in which rhythm and rhyme underpin emotion and the emphasis placed on contemporary poetry are all typical of Baudelaire's approach to reading, as his literary criticism makes clear, but what is also evident in this advice to the reader is the demands he places on us to set aside passive modes of consuming literature and become active partners, if not in the creative process, at least in the area of reception.

In addition to all this activity, Baudelaire closes his letter to Asselineau with the claim that he has 'written a long poem dedicated to Max Du Camp, destined to make nature and above all the lovers of progress shudder' (*c*, I, p. 553). This elliptical reference points to one of his greatest poems, the one that now closes *Les Fleurs du mal*, 'The Voyage'. Du Camp was a well-established figure in Paris's literary scene, one of the founders of the *Revue de Paris*, and widely known for his travel writing. His passion for modern inventions is evident from the fact that his account of his travels in Egypt, Nubia, Palestine and Asia Minor, published in 1851, was the first book to be illustrated with photographs. In 1855 he published *Les Chants modernes*, a collection of mediocre poems with a 40-page preface urging poets to sing of modernity and progress. Ours, he insists, is the century in which worlds and planets have been discovered, when uses have been found for steam, electricity, gas, chloroform, photography and so forth, and yet we are still expected to worry our heads about the Trojan War.[3] While his rejection of both the Pagan School and art for art's sake, together with his insistence on the inspirational value of modernity, have much in common with Baudelaire's, his naive belief in progress and his poems in which gas, steam and the locomotive all speak in the first person are far removed from the considerably more cynical views and the powerful rejection of the belief that material progress would inevitably lead to spiritual progress that we find both in Baudelaire's diaries and in 'The Voyage'. In an entry jotted down in *My Heart Laid Bare*, the 'confessions' he was working on during this period, Baudelaire refers to the 'theory of true civilization' as something which can be found neither in 'gas, nor in steam, nor in Ouija boards, but in the diminution of traces of original sin' (*oc*, I, p. 697). (The reference to Ouija boards indicates that the main focus of his criticism here is Victor Hugo, currently experimenting with means of contacting the dead.) The same conviction underpins 'The Voyage'. A poem in which the radiant optimism of departures (the child embarking on the journey of life, travellers setting out in hope of finding a better world) is rapidly crushed in darkness and a despairing recognition that all that awaits those who set out so hopefully is 'the tedious spectacle of immortal sin' (*oc*, I, p. 132), 'The Voyage' nevertheless ends with an image of light burning in the poet's heart and the ardent expectation that death will at least bring something new.

A few months later, at the end of April 1859, Baudelaire claimed in a letter to Poulet-Malassis that he had written some new *Fleurs du mal*, adding that they would be as destructive as a gas explosion in a glass shop (*c*, I, p. 568). Among these was 'The Head of Hair' which first appeared in *La Revue française* in May, and the two poems that appeared under the rubric: 'Parisian Phantoms' ('The Seven Old Men' and 'The Little Old Women), which *La Revue contemporaine* published on 15 September. These last two poems would form the nucleus of a new section of *Les Fleurs du mal*, the Parisian Pictures. But Baudelaire saw them as inaugurating not just a new thematic area but, more importantly, a radically different form of prosody. Writing to Jean Morel at the end of May, Baudelaire would describe 'The Seven Old Men' as the first of a new series he wanted to attempt, a poem in which he feared he had 'merely succeeded in going beyond the limits set down for Poetry' (*c*, I, p. 583). This combination of apparent modesty and underlying defiance is typical of Baudelaire, a characteristic rejection of the tastes and standards of the literary establishment whom he despised but realized he had to placate in order to have his work published at all. In dedicating the poems to Victor Hugo he both sets them under the aegis of a well-established poet, and draws his reader's attention to the considerable differences, thematic and stylistic, between Hugo's image of humanity and his own far bleaker one.

Following the 'method' he proclaimed to Calonne in a letter of November 1858, he embarked on various other tasks at the same time, pursuing his adaptation of De Quincey, writing a powerful article analysing the work of Théophile Gautier and also composing his account of the 1859 Salon, after what he claimed to Nadar was a single visit, bolstered by his memory and his knowledge of the artists listed in the catalogue. These, indeed, are years in which his diverse writings allow him to crystallize his image of art and the artist through studies of various different media: literary, visual and musical.

Baudelaire's essay on the poet, novelist and critic Gautier, for example, begins by setting aside the tight links between a writer's works and his biography that Sainte-Beuve's dominance as a literary critic had established as an essential starting point. Baudelaire sweeps Sainte-Beuve's approach aside with the claim that the most dramatic adventures in Gautier's life were those that took place 'under the dome of his brain', leaving the critic free to concentrate, not on banal dates and mere facts, but on the history of an obsession, that of an exclusive love of beauty. Obviously Baudelaire is using this essay in part to assert the dichotomy between his own life and the images revealed in his poems, what he terms their deliberate impersonality, a dichotomy the Tribunal had so signally failed to understand. The essay also allows him to cast a nostalgic and patriotic view back over the 'fertile crisis' of high French Romanticism, with some virtuoso displays of condensed descriptive writing: Chateaubriand, for instance, a generation older than most of the late Romantics, is like a star dropping down to the horizon, while Alexandre Dumas produced one after the other his fiery plays, 'whose volcanic eruptions were controlled with the dexterity of a skilful irrigator' (*oc*, II, p. 110).

Once more Baudelaire makes the distinction between morality and the task of literature, especially that of poetry. The principle of poetry, he reminds us yet again, is 'strictly and simply that of human aspiration towards a superior beauty', the implication being that morality and virtue have no place in such a process. Baudelaire also seizes on the opportunity to argue that beauty allows us to see the earth as a reflection of heaven, the real as a reflection of the ideal and, in particular, permits great poets, like great painters, to reveal the correspondences between the earthly and the heavenly, the stockpile, as he puts it, of all metaphor. This is why language should be perceived as something sacred and why those capable of the masterly manipulation of language practice thereby a kind of 'evocative magic' (*oc*, II, p. 118). Gautier's mastery of the language is such that he can claim, Baudelaire announces in an arresting formula, that 'anyone whom an idea, however subtle or unexpected, finds wanting, is no writer. The inexpressible does not exist' (*oc*, II, p. 118). Clearly Baudelaire was determined to show Gautier's mastery as both critic and creative writer, as if to cleanse him of any stains splashed on him by his connection with *Les Fleurs du mal*, but he has also seized on his article as a means of clarifying the nature and function of writing more generally.

In the same way, his review of the Salon of 1859 allowed him both to focus on those contemporary artists he most admired and to set down more general convictions concerning the nature of the plastic arts and more broadly still of creative production. His task was made easier by the paucity of great works on view at this particular Salon and the absence from it of the expected 'guests' from England, a lacuna he supplements with a brilliantly concise evocation of the themes he considers typical of that school:

> tragic passion, gestures in the vein of a Kean or a Macready
> [famous English tragedians], the intimate kindnesses of the
> *home*, oriental splendours reflected in the poetic mirror of the
> English mind, Scottish greenery, enchanting coolness, the

rapidly retreating depths of watercolours as vast as stage
scenery, although so small. (*oc*, II, p. 610)

Baudelaire links the absence of these works with what he perceives
as a general failure to appreciate imagination, which for him is the
queen of faculties, but which he considers has been replaced in the
minds of contemporary painters and public alike by mere technical
skill. Equally deplorable in his eyes, and closely associated with this
tendency, with its conviction that the role of art is to offer a faithful
reproduction of reality, was the rise of photography, which many
saw as a replacement for creative art. As a close friend of the great
photographer Félix Tournachon, known as Nadar, Baudelaire was
well aware of the creative and above all archival possibilities of
photography, its ability to save from oblivion 'the hanging ruins,
the books, prints and manuscripts that time devours' (*oc*, II, p.
618). What he deplores is both the slide of photography into
pornography, and the false appreciation of photography as capable
of entering into the domain of the 'impalpable and the imaginary,
into what has value only because the artist adds to it his own soul'
(*oc*, I, p. 619). Throughout his art criticism he has insisted that
what raises art from mere technical competence to greatness is the
way in which the artist's temperament and imagination interpret
and transform what is seen. Imagination, Baudelaire insists, is
capable both of the close-up, analytical view, and the synthetic
vision that pulls together elements that may have seemed disparate. It is what spurs all the other faculties into action, not just
the *sine qua non* of all great works of art, but essential also to war-
riors, diplomats and scholars.

In addition to his powerful exploration of the role of imagination, Baudelaire uses the opportunity of the Salon to explore the
work and thought of the contemporary painter he most admired,
Eugène Delacroix, set against the backdrop of other artists exhibit-
ing in the salon. Delacroix, he argues, is not merely an excellent

Eugène Delacroix,
Self-portrait, 1837,
oil on canvas.

draftsman, a prodigious colourist, an ardent and fertile creator of
images, but he rises above other artists because he is gifted with a
richer imagination, enabling him to express 'the intimate aspects
of the mind, the astonishing side of things . . . the infinite in the
finite', the vision that stems from an intense meditation (*oc*, ii,
pp. 636–7). That driving force of the imagination is also essential,
Baudelaire goes on to argue, in portrait painting, where the artist's
task is not just to represent the visible but also to 'guess what is
hidden' in order to represent 'a kind of dramatized biography'
(*oc*, ii, p. 655). In a similar way, the value of a landscape depends
not on the 'empty-headed cult of nature' but on 'the sentiment with
which the artist is able to imbue' the natural scene (*oc*, ii, p. 660),
the extent to which imagination has been able to purify and
explain raw nature. For Baudelaire, city-dweller as he was, nature's
value lay not in itself but in the 'prodigious reveries' it inspired

(*oc*, ii, p. 665). As so often happens in his critical writing, moreover, he seizes on a well-worn theme of landscape painting, in this case that of clouds, to flex his own writer's muscles, indicating in a passage of striking brilliance what could be done:

> in the end all those clouds with their fantastic and luminous shapes, that chaotic darkness, those immense areas of green and pink, hanging from or added to one another, those gaping furnaces, those firmaments of black or purple satin, dishevelled, rolled, or torn, those horizons in mourning or streaming with molten metal, all these depths, these splendours go to my head like an intoxicating drink or like the eloquence of opium. (*oc*, ii, p. 666)

The eloquence of opium: as we shall see, his adaptation of De Quincey had certainly brought home to him the powerful rhetorical devices that the English writer had deployed in revealing both the pleasures and the pains of this artificial stimulant.

Even sculpture, that 'singular art whose roots go back into the darkness of time', which Baudelaire had summarily dismissed in his earlier art criticism, furnishes him with the pretext for some particularly intense writing in the 'Salon of 1859', as he surveys the diverse ways in which statues in modern life, in libraries, gardens, and public squares, force the viewer to 'meditate on things that are not of this earth' (*oc*, ii, p. 670). Yet again, what he seeks out in sculpture as in all other forms of art is proof of that powerful imagination that allows the sculptor to transcend the material and represent phantoms 'full of the void' and 'tumultuous dreams'. (*oc*, ii, pp. 678, 680)

It is also in this review of the Salon that he devotes a passage to the cityscapes of Charles Meryon, prints of which he had begged Asselineau to scrounge for him some months earlier. 'Through the harshness, refinement, and sureness of his drawing, M. Meryon

Charles Meryon,
*Hôtel Dieu, Paris
before its Destruction
in 1850*, undated
etching.

recalls the excellent etchers of the past', Baudelaire claims, going
on to assert:

> I have rarely seen the natural solemnity of a vast city represented
> with more poetry. The majesty of massed stone, spires 'pointing
> to the sky', the obelisks of industry vomiting to the firmament
> their accumulations of smoke, the prodigious scaffolding of
> monuments under repair, applying to the solid body of the
> architecture their own openwork architecture with its highly
> paradoxical beauty, the turbulent sky, freighted with rage and
> rancour, the depth of perspectives increased by the thought of
> all the dramas that have unfolded within them, none of the
> complex elements that make up the grim and glorious decor
> of civilization has been forgotten. (*oc*, ii, pp. 666–7)

In early 1860 Baudelaire would hope to join forces with Meryon to produce poetic descriptions of these illustrations, 'the philosophical reveries of someone strolling through Paris', something no doubt like the prose poems. But as he wryly explained to Poulet-Malassis:

> M. Meryon doesn't see things like that. You have to say: on the right, you see this; on the left you see that. You have to seek out notes in old books. You have to say: here there were initially twelve windows, reduced to ten by the artist, and finally you have to go to the Town Hall to find out the exact date of the demolitions. M. Meryon speaks, his eyes on the ceiling, without listening to any remarks you might make to him. (*c*, I, p. 670)

Nevertheless, the very thought of such a collaboration was useful in helping frame Baudelaire's image of the prose poems, whose radically different literary form and contemporary images he described as being born from 'frequenting enormous cities, from the crisscrossing of their countless connections' (*oc*, I, p. 276).

Early 1860 was remarkable for several other events in Baudelaire's life. On the first day of the New Year he sold Poulet-Malassis and De Broise the second edition of *Les Fleurs du mal*, which would be published in February of the following year. The second half of the month saw the publication of his adaptation of De Quincey's *Confessions of an English Opium Eater*. One of the reasons for his fascination with this work is explained in his 'Hashish Poem', which would appear a few months later, when it forms a kind of preamble to the *Confessions*. There are days, he tells us in the 'Hashish Poem', in a formula he repeats elsewhere, when we wake up feeling that our intelligence is 'youthful and vigorous', when the outside world offers itself to us in 'powerful relief', with an admirable 'clarity of contour and richness of colour'. The moral world 'opens up its vast perspectives, full of new revelations' (*oc*, I,

p. 401). The problem is that there seems no way of bringing this state of mind about through an act of will. Its arbitrary nature makes it seem more like 'a veritable act of grace', a 'magic mirror' in which we are invited to see ourselves as we could and should be (*oc*, I, p. 402). Because such a state of mind is so conducive to producing great works of art, Baudelaire argues, there is a strong temptation to induce it artificially, through drugs like alcohol, hashish and opium. As a result, in exploring the effect of these drugs Baudelaire is also, in effect, analysing the working of the creative imagination at its most powerful.

He acknowledges that the study of opium has already been done, 'so arrestingly, in such a medical and poetic way' (*oc*, I, p. 403), that all he needs to do is to investigate that work, the confessions of the English Romantic writer, Thomas De Quincey. But while he claims that there is no need for him to add anything to De Quincey's work, he does in fact insert many of his own comments and insights, and he transforms the order in which the writer set out his experiences. Most strikingly, Baudelaire chose to begin the work with a stirring passage that the author himself had buried away deep within his confessions, a passage to which Baudelaire would give the heading 'Précautions oratoires' – a standard phrase meaning 'carefully phrased remarks' but having here also the force of an eloquent warning:

> Oh! just, subtle, and mighty opium! that to the hearts of poor
> and rich alike, for the wounds that will never heal, and for
> 'the pangs that tempt the spirit to rebel' bringest an assuaging
> balm; eloquent opium! that with thy potent rhetoric stealest
> away the purposes of wrath; and to the guilty man, for one
> night givest back the hopes of his youth, and hands washed
> pure from blood; and to the proud man, a brief oblivion for
>   Wrongs unredress'd and insults unavenged;
> that summonest to the chancery of dreams, for the triumphs of

suffering innocence, false witnesses; and confoundest perjury; and dost reverse the sentences of unrighteous judges; – thou buildest upon the bosom of the darkness, out of the fantastic imagery of the brain, cities and temples, beyond the art of Phidias and Praxiteles – beyond the splendour of Babylon and Hekatómpylos: and 'from the anarchy of dreaming sleep', callest into sunny light the faces of long-buried beauties, and the blessed household countenances, cleansed from the 'dishonours of the grave'. Thou only givest these gifts to man; and thou has the keys of Paradise, oh, just, subtle, and mighty opium! (*MOP*, p. 101)

In much of this Baudelaire must have seen reflections of his own dreams and his own poetry: the chancery of dreams dominates 'The Ragpicker's Wine'; 'Parisian Dream' builds a fantastic city 'on the bosom of darkness'; blessed household countenances are briefly returned to the world in 'I Have Not Forgotten' and 'The Great-Hearted Servant'. To some extent, indeed, adapting De Quincey's exploration of opium allowed Baudelaire to offer a metaphorical exploration of his own creative imagination as well as that of all great artists. After all, in a brief portrait which is at the same time a self-portrait, he indicates that the focus of attention here is the drug's effect on 'a subtle and educated mind, an ardent and cultivated imagination, above all one that has been prematurely ploughed over by fertilising grief' (*MOP*, p. 104), and in a phrase inserted into De Quincey's text Baudelaire refers to opium-takers as 'a contemplative nation lost within the active nation' (*MOP*, p. 102). Similar insertions, drawing understated but unmistakable parallels between himself and De Quincey, occur elsewhere in the adaptation. At one point, for instance, Baudelaire comments: 'to feel like that, one has to have greatly suffered, to be one of those hearts that misfortune opens and softens, unlike those whose hearts it closes and hardens. The Bedouin of civilization learns in the Sahara of great cities many causes for compassion that are unknown to the man whose sensitivity is limited by home and family' (*MOP*, p. 132). Like Baudelaire himself, the opium eater is presented, in another insertion into the original text, as longing to 'plunge into the heart of the multitude of the disinherited' (*MOP*, p. 156). The reader is advised to take note of a Malaysian whom De Quincey encounters: 'he will reappear,' Baudelaire warns us, 'multiplied in a terrible way, for who can calculate what power of reflection and repercussion an incident can have in the life of a dreamer?' (*MOP*, p. 168). The old man the poet encounters in 'The Seven Old Men' and who reappears in a further six avatars is close kin to De Quincey's Malaysian. Above all, the passages in which De Quincey refers to opium's power to sap the will find telling commentaries in Baudelaire's version:

> Horrible situation! To have a mind teeming with ideas and to be unable to cross the bridge that separates the imaginary coun-tries of reverie from the positive harvests of action! If those who read me now have ever needed to produce something, I don't need to describe for them the despair of a noble, clear-sighted, gifted mind, struggling against that very particular damnation. An abominable enchantment! Everything I have said about the weakening of willpower in my study on hashish is applicable to opium. (*MOP*, p. 180)

Fearing that De Quincey's style would be too digressive, as he terms it, for the French mind, stamped with Cartesian logic and formed by the clarity of expression that dominates French Classicism, Baudelaire condensed and reorganized his text, giving it a 'dramatic shape' as he said to Poulet-Malassis (*C*, I, p. 669), and producing a translation that is in its own way an act both of criticism and of creativity.

At the end of 1860 he would agree, for purely financial reasons, to translate part of Longfellow's lengthy poem *Hiawatha* for the composer R. Stoepfel, who, moreover, decamped without paying him for his work. While the *Hiawatha* translation may not be more than competent, Baudelaire's translations of Poe and De Quincey, two writers in whom he found many parallels with his own thinking, produced work of the very highest calibre, work that is also a 'magic mirror' reflecting much of his own thinking.

Working on De Quincey's *Confessions* seems to have inspired him to write his own 'confessions'. In a letter to his mother in April 1861 he mentioned 'a large book I've been dreaming about for the last two years'. He gave this work the title *My Heart Laid Bare* and continued to refer to it until 1865. It would be in this work that he would register all his sources of anger, producing something so searing that in comparison the *Confessions* of Jean-Jacques Rousseau would pale into insignificance (*c*, II, p. 182, 302), something that would be so full of rancour, impertinence and revenge that it would be impossible to publish until he had accumulated a fortune sufficient to place him beyond the reach of those he had offended (*c*, II, p. 305). Although he would never complete this project, he did gather numerous notes for it. While some of these are suggestions for topics that could be expanded, others concern the nature of the venture itself. 'I can begin *My Heart Laid Bare* at any point, in any way, and continue it day by day, according to the inspiration of the day and of the circumstances', he urges himself in one entry, adding: 'all that matters is that the inspiration should be energetic' (*oc*, I, p. 677). 'You have to work,' he urges himself at one point, 'if not through taste, at least through despair, because, when everything has been taken into account, work is less boring than amusement' (*oc*, I, p. 682). There are notes for a study of dandies, for a history of his translation of Poe, and for portraits and anecdotes about his contemporaries, as well as for a virulent attack on the writer George Sand. To understand this fury with George Sand we need to bear in mind first the personal context, in which Baudelaire's request that she promote the actress Marie

Daubrun was turned down, through no fault of George Sand's, but to Baudelaire's chagrin and anger. In addition, there was the more intellectual point concerning her rejection of the concept of hell, one of the under-girding premises of *Les Fleurs du mal*. Occasionally the notes seem to suggest the desire to transform into a different genre a poem that he had already written, as when he takes up the central theme of 'L'Héautontimorouménos': 'it would be sweet to be turn and turn about the victim and the torturer' (*oc*, I, p. 676), proclaim the notes, while the poem insists:

> I am the wound, I am the knife,
> I am the blow and I'm the cheek,
> I am the limbs and I'm the wheel,
> Torturer and victim both am I. (*oc*, I, p. 79)

In other passages he focuses on political events – his own 'intoxication' in 1848, the horrors of the June uprisings, his rage at Napoleon III's *coup d'état* (*oc*, I, p. 679) – and explores both torture and the death penalty. He takes aim at well-known critics, and derides bourgeois values ('to be a useful man has always struck me as something very hideous') (*oc*, I, p. 679). The art of divination seems to have aroused his interest at one point, just as commerce incurred his ire, and the nature of colloquial language attracted his attention as an indication of hidden tendencies of the communal mind. Whether with more time Baudelaire might have turned this into a study putting Rousseau's *Confessions* in the shade is questionable, but the light it sheds on his interests, passions and irritations nevertheless makes it a valuable document, frequently quoted by Baudelaire scholars, but demanding a sharp awareness of the context that provoked it.

In February 1860 he attended a concert of Richard Wagner's music, whose intensity and power overwhelmed him, as he confessed in a letter to the composer, a letter moreover that amounted, as he put it, to a 'cry of thanks' (*c*, I, p. 672). Wagner must have been all the more delighted to receive this enthusiastic response to his music, in that so much of the French public, as well as many French critics, had greeted his work with incomprehension and hostility. In his letter Baudelaire paid Wagner a compliment that recalls his first reaction on reading Poe: at first, he says, 'it seemed to me that I knew that music and then thinking it over later, I understood the source of this mirage; it seemed to me that the music was *my own*, and that I recognized it as every one recognizes things they are destined to love' (*c*, I, p. 673). He would even plan to visit Vienna in September 1861 to hear more of the composer's music with his friend Champfleury, another admirer of Wagner. Instead he devoted to Wagner his only article of music criticism, 'Richard Wagner and *Tannhäuser* in Paris', published on 1 April 1861 in the *Revue européenne.* Once again, he insists in this article on the value and the necessity of imagination not just in the artist but also in the audience. 'In music, as in painting and in the written word,' Baudelaire argues, 'there is always a gap to be filled in by the listener's imagination' (*oc*, II, p. 782). His own imagination being primarily visual, his essay, like his letter, draws frequently on the language of painting and colour to explore the effects created by musical sounds, just as he sets the confrontation in *Tannhäuser* in terms of his own dualism, representing it as 'the struggle between two principles that have chosen the human heart for their main battle ground, the struggle between the flesh and the mind, hell and heaven, Satan and God' (*oc*, II, p. 794).

It was in February 1860, just after writing to Wagner, that he began a correspondence with a young critic, Armand Fraisse, who had dared to write an admiring review of *Les Fleurs du mal* in 1857 and who had recently included in one of his reviews a warm tribute to Baudelaire's outstanding originality. In his letter Baudelaire not only insists on 'the labour needed to transform a reverie into a work of art' but also gives his unforgettable justification for writing sonnets:

because the form is constricting, the idea bursts forth all the more intensely. Everything suits the Sonnet, buffoonery, gallantry, passion, reverie, philosophical meditation. It has the beauty of finely wrought metal and mineral. Have you observed how a patch of sky, seen through a vent, or between two chimneys or two rocks, or through an arcade etc., gives a deeper idea of the infinite than the great panorama seen from a mountain top? (*c*, I, p. 676)

The fact that he took the time to write to an unknown indicates how much energy he still enjoyed at this point, an indication further borne out by his continuing to produce ideas for future projects. For instance, he started jotting down ideas for a projected study of literary dandies, men who constantly worked to create the image of themselves that they wanted the public to perceive. Still eager to make his mark in the theatre, he drew up plans for a play based on a short story by one of those dandies, Paul de Molènes. His continuing interest in the theatre may well have been further stimulated by his growing awareness of Wagner's image of the genre as a *Gesamtkunstwerk*, succinctly evoked in Baudelaire's article on the composer in these terms: 'dramatic art, that is to say the reunion or *coincidence* of several arts' (*oc*, II, p. 782).

While he would never complete either of these projects, he did produce a series of literary studies for Eugène Crépet's anthology of French poets. The anthology consists of a series of essays, accompanied by a selection of poems by the writer under discussion. Crépet was six years Baudelaire's junior, sufficiently well off to live on the returns from his investments, a republican by conviction, sharing the assurance held by many of his generation, including most vocally Hugo, and rejected most vocally by Baudelaire, that material progress would inevitably lead to moral progress. A staunch patriot, he was eager to promote French literature, so much so that he paid for the publication of *Les Poëtes français* from his own pocket.

To represent the Romantic period in his anthology, as Baudelaire explains in a letter of 15 May 1862, Crépet drew on the suggestions of Asselineau, Philoxène Boyer and Baudelaire himself, who supplied a detailed list of poets who should be included. Asselineau wrote 28 of the articles, while Boyer added thirteen, but Baudelaire's seven articles included five on the most prominent writers of the period: Victor Hugo, Théophile Gautier, Marceline Desbordes-Valmore, Théodore de Banville and Leconte de Lisle. He had originally planned to write ten, but one of these was rejected by Crépet, shocked by a line in which Baudelaire, thinking back to his youthful friendship with the poet in question, Gustave Le Vavasseur, and wanting to compare his experiments in verse with his gymnastic prowess, recalled coming into his friend's room and finding him performing various physical feats 'almost naked' (*oc*, II, p. 180). Baudelaire was furious that his article was rejected, and his rage was further exacerbated when he was not sent a copy of the published volume, on the grounds that he had not yet returned some books by Hugo that Crépet had lent him. For all that, Crépet would go on to publish a well-researched biographical study of the poet, and he and his son Jacques Crépet helped launch the re-evaluation that would eventually lead to Baudelaire's present-day appreciation.

Most importantly, the project itself produced some of Baudelaire's finest literary criticism and, by giving him a forum for exploring some of the most pressing critical and creative questions confronting him, enabled readers to enter into the artist's studio that, in his proposed preface to *Les Fleurs du mal*, he had been so reluctant to open to us. His article on Hugo, for instance, allowed him to explore the question of analogies between the external world and the moral world, between objects and human vices and virtues. 'What is pure art according to the modern concept of it?', he asks in his note for the article on philosophical art. The answer he supplies coincides with the argument in the Hugo article: 'It is the creation of a suggestive magic containing both object and subject, the world beyond the artist and the artist himself' (*oc*, II, p. 598). Like several of the other articles, moreover, it gave him the opportunity to flex his writing muscles by producing a pastiche of Hugo's own literary style. The following passage, for instance, picks up on Hugo's fascination with the cosmos and his penchant for accumulating not merely images but also rhetorical questions:

> You germinations, blossomings, flowerings, eruptions, successive or simultaneous, slow or sudden, progressive or complete, of planets, stars, suns, constellations, are you simply forms of the life of God, or dwelling places prepared by His goodness or His justice for souls He wishes to educate or bring progressively closer to Himself? Worlds eternally studied, perhaps forever unknown, oh! say, do you contain paradises, hells, purgatories, prisons, villas, palaces and so forth? If new systems and groupings, assuming unexpected shapes, adopting unforeseen combinations, undergoing laws never yet registered, imitating all the providential caprices of a geometry too vast and too complicated for human compass, were to leap from the limbo of the future, what would there be in that thought that is so *exorbitant*, so monstrous, as to exceed the legitimate limits of poetic conjecture? (*oc*, II, p. 138)

In writing on the poet Marceline Desbordes-Valmore, who produced the first volume of French poetry that can truly be called Romantic, Baudelaire, despite his dislike of women writers and while registering his disapproval of her prosodic errors, finds himself forced to admire the intensity and eloquence of her writing, the sense of spontaneity she conveys, her ability to make the reader believe that nothing comes between her and the direct expression of emotion. Moreover, he concludes with a pastiche of her writing that he justifies by arguing that he has always taken pleasure in 'seeking out in external and visible nature examples and metaphors

that would serve to characterize pleasures and impressions of a
spiritual nature' (*oc*, II, p. 148). Clearly this search also underpins
much of his creative writing. In turning to his long-time friend, the
lyric poet Banville, he suggests a critical approach that consists in
seeking out the word a poet most frequently uses as a key to understanding the work as a whole. In Banville's case, he argues, that
word is lyre, a word that expresses 'that almost supernatural state,
that intensity of existence in which the soul *sings*, in which it is
almost *forced to sing*' (*oc*, II, p. 164). Other articles give him the
opportunity to imply that the true value of poetry can be found
not in any desire to 'illuminate the people and to use rhyme and
number to fix scientific discoveries more easily in human memory'
(*oc*, II, p. 145), but in pursuing beauty for its own sake, or to argue

that 'the law of work' (*oc*, ii, p. 161) rather than the mere exploitation of a gift, is what guarantees true poetic glory. While the articles themselves are relatively short, taken as a whole they nevertheless provide illuminating insights not just into the poetry of Baudelaire's time but also into his own concept of both creative and critical writing. And examined against the background of what other critics were writing about the same authors, they also reveal how deeply Baudelaire was engaged in the central aesthetic and ethical debates of his time, how aware he was of contemporary literary issues and how much his critical vocabulary is coloured by that of the critics of his day.

These are years that also see Baudelaire adding to his friends and acquaintances. He began building up a friendship with the man on whom he would base his depiction of the painter of modern life, Constantin Guys, with whom he hoped create a fine illustrated

Edouard Manet,
Baudelaire, 1862,
engraving.

143

edition of the works of Poe. Sometime in the late 1850s, he met the painter who would become one of his closest friends and strongest supporters, Edouard Manet, to whom we owe a beautiful profile of the poet. And the actress, spy and 'beautiful adventuress' Elisa Neri (La Sisina), who was a friend of Apollonie Sabatier, inspired him to draft the following plan for a novel, tentatively called *The Rational Madman and the Beautiful Adventuress*:

> Sensual pleasure in the Society of the Extravagant.
> What horror and what delight in the love for a spy, a thief, etc.!
> The moral cause of this pleasure.
> It's always necessary to return to De Sade, that is to *Natural Man*, to explain evil.
> Begin with a conversation, on love between difficult people.
> Monstrous feelings of friendship or admiration for a depraved woman.
> All of Sisina is in this.
> Imagine horrible, strange adventures, across capital cities.
> (*oc*, I, pp. 595–6)

While he would never complete this project, he did write a poem for her, publishing it in the *Revue française* in April 1859. There he sets up a series of oxymorons to suggest the complexity of this surprising woman, whom he sees as a 'gentle warrior' whose soul is as 'charitable' as that of a murderess, a woman whose heart has been ravaged by fire but who, for a lover worthy of it, always possesses a 'reservoir of tears' (*oc*, I, p. 61). Her image therefore contributes to the complex vision of woman conveyed by Baudelaire's prose and verse poetry, one that is inescapably marked by the misogyny of the time and by his own sense, dating back to childhood, that his mother had rejected him, but that is remarkably wide-ranging for all its isolation within a lonely masculinism.

Two curious and atypical events mark the year 1861. The first concerns Baudelaire's brief acceptance of a disciple, Léon Cladel, whom he helped with a short story, 'Aux amours éternelles' helping him purge it of 'half-a-dozen improper terms' (*c*, II, p. 184), and a novel, *Les Martyrs ridicules*, for which Baudelaire wrote a preface and which Cladel dedicated to him. Poulet-Malassis, who published this novel, later commented on the relationship in a letter to Albert de la Fizelière, who, together with Georges Decaux, published the first biography of Baudelaire, in 1868: 'Baudelaire, on my recommendation, took an interest in this young man, which did not last long. This southerner, like many of his compatriots, is a bit of a *poseur*. But all the same, *Les Martyrs ridicules* was *completely revised and reworked in line with Baudelaire's suggestions*' (*OC*, II, p. 1165). Baudelaire seized on the opportunity of the preface to write a scathing evaluation of contemporary French youth, among which he distinguishes four types: the first caring about nothing but fornication and food; the second thinking of nothing but money; the third *'aspiring to make the populace happy'* (*OC*, II, p. 182), and thus incurring Baudelaire's rage by recalling his own fleeting hopes in 1848; and the fourth devoting themselves to realist art and literature, and hating museums and libraries. How did this group come about, Baudelaire wonders, invoking, in the wake of the great naturalist Buffon, the idea of spontaneous generation: 'This group must have been born of itself, spontaneously, like the infinitely small in a jug of putrid water, the great French jug' (*OC*, II, p. 183). Baudelaire uses his attack on this group to promote one of his deeply held and irascibly expressed beliefs:

On their absolute confidence in genius and inspiration, they base their right not to undergo any kind of gymnastics. They are unaware that geniuses (if indeed one can use this word for the indefinable seed of the great man) must, like the apprentice acrobat, risk breaking their bones a thousand times in secret before dancing before the public; that inspiration, to be brief, is nothing but the reward for daily exercise. (*oc*, II, p. 183)

As for Realism, he would affirm that reality is not the mere copying of nature but what is created by visionaries. What attracted him to Cladel's novel, he claims, was the writer's determination to depict this 'lamentable cast' with rancorous energy. But there are other reasons too, reasons associated with his own situation, for when the central character accepts his failure and turns back to the 'salutary impressions of childhood' and particularly to his mother, 'that lap always open to *drop outs*' (*oc*, II, p. 187) there can be no doubt that Baudelaire was reminded of himself and his own mother, whose lap was not particularly open and whose purse was all too often closed.

Cladel was quickly dropped from Baudelaire's close acquaintances, but the episode left its trace on one of the prose poems, 'Loss of a Halo', which was first offered for publication (but rejected) in 1865. The central figure in this poem tells a friend how he lost his halo while crossing a busy boulevard, and was too anxious, what with all the traffic, that 'moving chaos where death arrives at the gallop from all sides at once', to go back and pick it up. When his friend urges him to advertise its loss, the poet, happy with the anonymity that allows him to hang out in low dives, replies:

Certainly not! I'm quite content here. You're the only one who recognized me. What's more, dignity bores me. And then, what fun to think of some bad poet picking it up and impudently putting it on. Think of making someone happy, what a delight! and particularly someone who would make me laugh! Think of x or z! Hey, wouldn't that be funny! (*oc*, I, p. 352)

A Cladel donning Baudelaire's reputation clearly struck him as a source of unexpected and enjoyable comedy.

Then, at the end of 1861, Baudelaire embarked on one of the strangest episodes in his life. Despite his frequent expressions of scorn for public honours, he decided to seek admittance to the French Academy, that elite group of 40, each chosen by those already in the Academy, whose primary purpose was to preserve the purity of the French language. Certainly Baudelaire had snorted in his preface to *Les Martyrs ridicules* that 'grammar will soon be something as forgotten as reason, and at the rate at which we are walking towards the shadows, there is cause to hope that in the year 1900 we will be plunged in total darkness' (*oc*, ii, p. 183). Nevertheless, it is hard to imagine that he really thought he would be accepted by such a profoundly conservative body, one moreover that could be guaranteed to look with horror and scorn on a poet whose works had been judged offensive to public and religious morals. Not surprisingly, he soon realized how small his chances were and withdrew in mid-February, but in the process of visiting academicians and others who might help him he encountered one unexpectedly sympathetic supporter, the poet Alfred de Vigny, unfortunately already suffering from the stomach cancer that would kill him in December 1863. Vigny's letter of 27 January 1862, inviting Baudelaire to visit him, advised him not to waste his name and his 'true and rare talent' in what he terms the Labyrinth (his capital L) of a candidacy for the Academy, but must have poured balm on the poet's raw nerves in his assessment of *Les Fleurs du mal*:

I have read and reread you and need to tell you how much these *flowers of evil* are, for me, *flowers of good* that charm me. How much too I find you unjust towards this bouquet which is often so delightfully perfumed with spring scents, to have imposed on it this title which is unworthy of it, and how much I bear you a grudge for having in it something poisoned with what I can only call emanations from Hamlet's graveyard . . . What you can't know is the pleasure with which I read to others, to Poets, the true beauties of your poems, which are still appreciated too little and judged too superficially.[4]

If he found in Vigny an unforeseen admirer, however, Baudelaire was to discover yet again how little his old friend Sainte-Beuve appreciated him. Urged by the poet to support his candidature, Sainte-Beuve wrote an article for the establishment paper *Le Constitutionnel* of 20 January 1862, entitled 'On the upcoming elections to the Academy', in which he maliciously described Baudelaire, in a passage that has become infamous, as having constructed a bizarre kiosk 'at the far point of Romanticism's Kamschatka peninsula, which I call *Baudelaire's Folly*'.[5] Although Baudelaire proclaimed himself 'more tickled than scratched' (*c*, II, p. 219) by this judgement, an article he published anonymously in the *Revue anecdotique*, and in which he sums up the eminent critic's views, suggests rather that he decided to make as much as he could of the publicity, however condescending. Another article, this time in a journal Baudelaire detested, *Le Siècle*, and written by Edmond Texier (to whom, as editor of *L'Illustration*, he would send his article on Constantin Guys, only to have it returned months later) also mentioned Baudelaire, this time as 'an audacious poet' who, were he to enter the sacred precincts of the Academy, would make its windows shatter into a thousand pieces, unless the god of classical tradition were already dead and buried (*c*, II, p. 762). Baudelaire may well have had this judgement in mind when, a few months later, he published his prose poem 'The Bad Glazier' with its images of shattered glass. In any case, his attempt to enter the Academy cannot but strike us as one of those crises he describes in this prose poem, 'which justify our belief that malicious Demons slip into us and make us carry out, unbeknown to us, their most absurd desires' (*oc*, I, p. 286).

This was a time when Baudelaire, increasingly harassed by debtors, was also made ever more aware of human mortality. In

Charles-Augustin
Sainte-Beuve,
c. 1860.

May 1859 Jeanne had been struck down by an attack of paralysis, and less than a year later his half-brother Alphonse fell seriously ill as a result of a stroke. Alphonse would die on 14 April 1862, aged only 51. While he had all but ignored his brother for years, this illness offered an ominous warning for Baudelaire himself. In a note jotted down in *Hygiene*, he remarks:

> Both morally and physically, I have always had the sensation of the chasm, not just that of sleep, but that of action, dream, memory, desire, regret, remorse, beauty, number etc. I cultivated my

hysteria with joy and terror. Now I constantly suffer from vertigo, and today, 23 January 1862, I have had a singular warning. I felt pass over me the *wind of the wing of imbecility*. (*OC*, I, p. 668)

This was the first of the apoplectic attacks that would eventually destroy him. We should note the word he chooses: imbecility, not madness. There is no tint of Romanticism here, nothing of that school's belief in madness as a means of gaining special insights into existence. Etymologically an imbecile is one who lacks the support of a stick, forced to stagger along unsupported. The stick is intelligence, and Baudelaire's analytical mind foresaw what lay in wait for him and noted it down, perceiving it as something deeply rooted within him, but also something he himself had cultivated, perhaps considering that here too there were parallels with Poe, whose drinking he believed had also been cultivated with joy and terror.

5

The Final Years

The dandy, Baudelaire suggests, 'must ceaselessly aspire to be sublime; he must live and sleep in front of a mirror', the kind of mental mirror, in fact, offered by such notebooks as *My Heart Laid Bare* (*oc*, I, p. 678). He is not thinking so much of the outward appearance, which is merely 'a symbol of the aristocratic superiority of [the dandy's] mind', as of 'a kind of religion', the 'last glow of heroism in a decadent world', an ardent desire for originality and, above all, an essential characteristic of the artist of modern life (*oc*, II, p. 710). The concept of the dandy implies, he argues, 'a quintessence of character, and a subtle understanding of the entire moral mechanism of this world' (*oc*, II, p. 691). Over time, he contends in 'The Painter of Modern Life', the idea we have of beauty subtly penetrates our clothes, our gestures and our face. Through an effort of will, the dandy comes to 'resemble what [he] would like to be' (*oc*, II, p. 684). What image of himself, one wonders, had Baudelaire managed to fashion by the beginning of the 1860s?

As a frequenter of cafés and cabarets, as well as an habitué of the bureaux attached to various journals – two aspects of city life that he missed during his brief stays at Honfleur – Baudelaire is mirrored in the memoirs of several of his contemporaries. Catulle Mendès, the dynamic editor of the *Revue fantaisiste*, perceptively describes him as slender, elegant, somewhat shifty, almost frightening because of his vaguely frightened attitude, haughty moreover, but gracefully so, exerting that seductive charm possessed by anything that is both attractive and horrifying, he recalled a very delicate and slightly damned bishop who had dressed for a voyage in exquisite secular clothes: His Eminence Mylord Brummel.[1]

The writer Lorédan Larchey left a brief but remarkable pen portrait:

His hair was closely cropped, and his head rose straight up from a kind of red wool fabric half hidden by the raised collar of his overcoat. His face, completely shaved, was as angular and bony as that of an ascetic, with regular features. Under the ridge of his eyebrows, two black, sharply piercing eyes gleamed with a special light, the only things that animated a man who seemed frozen in his shell.[2]

The prolific writer Philibert Audebrand, who had known Baudelaire from the mid-1840s when they both worked on the journal *Le Corsaire-Satan*, recalled him at this later stage of their lives in his book *Un Café de journalistes sous Napoléon iii*, published in 1888. There he described the Baudelaire of the early 1860s as

aged, faded, weighed down although still slim, an eccentric with white hair and a face always shaved, looking less like a poet of bitter pleasures than a priest of Saint-Sulpice [Church]. Not having lost the habitude of playing the misanthropist, he would sit down on his own at a small table and call for a jug of beer and a pipe that he filled with tobacco, lit, and smoked, all without saying a word throughout the whole evening.[3]

The writer and journalist Charles Yriarte, whose chapter devoted to the poet in his *Portraits cosmopolites* quotes extensively from him, sometimes without acknowledgement, paints a more appealing picture of him as a man 'who struck a perfect note':

> in talking to him, you felt you were in the company of something pungent and strong; but the writer was silent and reserved when he was not intimately acquainted with those speaking to him, and in that case he would speak little, expressing himself quietly, very slowly, articulating his words precisely, sculpting his phrases and rounding out his sentences. He read as a priest officiates, somewhat solemnly, but with a rare perfection, and it was a treat to hear him read his sonnets, some of which are masterpieces of style. He had very fine features, and never abandoned himself to a hearty, loud laugh, but his thin lips would fold in a smile. He had something of the priest and the artist in him, something strange and inexplicable too that was in accordance with the nature of his talent and the extravagant habits of his life.[4]

That Yriarte may well have been the victim of some of Baudelaire's famous leg-pulling where those extravagant habits were concerned is suggested by the fact that he affirms not just that in his youth Baudelaire had visited India, but also that he had read 45 volumes of Balzac during the crossing.[5]

Another of his café friends, the writer and publisher Gabriel de Gonet, divulges that Baudelaire was passionately fond of the game of billiards, revealing an unexpected determination to succeed even in the most difficult of plays. Life has only one real charm, Baudelaire notes in *Fusées*: 'the charm of Gambling. But what if we do not care whether we win or lose?' (*OC*, I, p. 654). It is easy to see in this fascination with billiards a parallel with his poem depicting gamblers who find, in the random luck of the cards or fall of the dice, a way of forgetting the harsh reality of bills, creditors and deadlines. It was this reality that would begin to press even harder

on him in the years immediately following the great burst of energetic activity that marks the end of the 1850s. Its ravages were
reflected in a portrait that embellished Poulet-Malassis' new Paris
headquarters when they opened in late 1860 or early 1861.
Alexandre Lafont's medallion of Baudelaire shows the head of the
40-year-old poet against a greenish background, his hair growing
thin around the brow, but falling in waves to his shoulders, deep
lines around nose and mouth, chin up and lower lip thrust slightly
forward, his eyes gazing at us with an intense blend of defiance and
distrust, combined with a hint of sorrow.

There was good reason for both sorrow and anger in these early
years of the decade. His financial difficulties were growing more and
more serious, mired as he was in high-interest debts entered into in
order to service previous loans. In October 1860 he went to Honfleur
in the hope that his mother would either agree to abandon the *conseil judiciaire* or lend him enough money to help him out of his increasingly pressing financial difficulties. She herself, however, was in
some difficulty as a result of having to make essential repairs on the
Honfleur house, and he was forced to return to what he called the
hell of Paris (*c*, ii, p. 101), desperate to find a way of extracting himself from the descending spiral of debts, loans and promissory notes.

To make matters worse, he still felt financially responsible for
Jeanne Duval, whose reprobate brother (who may well not have
been a brother at all, but a former or even current lover) also
expected to live on the money the financially embattled Baudelaire
gave his erstwhile mistress. Frequently drunk, ill and partially
paralysed, and, at least according to Baudelaire, incapable of sharing any of his intellectual or artistic interests, she was still able to
inspire a poem that suggests how powerfully the poet continued to
remember past passion despite present bitterness. 'A Phantom',
which he sent to Poulet-Malassis in early March 1860, consists of
four loosely connected sonnets. In the first, he depicts himself
plunged in caverns of immeasurable sorrow, a painter forced to

paint on darkness, but whose loneliness is from time to time broken by a 'beautiful visitor' who is both dark and full of light. The second sonnet evokes the power of memory to recall lost moments, while the third remembers how the beloved's beauty was enhanced by the clothes, jewels and furniture that surrounded her. The last sonnet offers us a portrait that again proclaims the power of memory to protect against the decay inflicted by time, here personified as a destructive old man, who, the poet boldly asserts, may destroy the lovers' physical beings but never the poet's recollections of the woman who was his pleasure and his glory. While in the new edition the cycle of poems inspired by her would close on one he had already included in the 1857 edition, this poem, with its sharp awareness of the ravages of time, and its determination to cling to memories of a happier past, together with the exotic and erotic 'The Head of Hair', first published in May 1859, make the picture he has left of her far more complex and far richer than the poems of his passionate youth. Moreover, they bring to the foreground an aspect that was becoming increasingly important in Baudelaire's aesthetics, the role of memory, that powerful tool in the extraction of symbol and metaphor from lived experience, and in the transposition of mere ephemeral reality into the permanence of art.

In August 1860, as Baudelaire was preparing his new edition of *Les Fleurs du mal* for publication, he longed to include an allegorical frontispiece that would stimulate his readers' visual memories and suggest the need for a similar transposition on their part. What he wanted was something like the *Dance of Death* he had found in a work by the early nineteenth-century artist Eustache-Hyacinthe Langlois. Writing to Nadar in May 1859 Baudelaire had described what he sought: 'a skeleton in the form of a tree, legs and ribs forming the trunk, arms outstretched and bursting into leaves and buds, as it protects several rows of poisonous plants in little pots lined up as if in a gardener's hothouse' (c, I, p. 577). Unfortunately, Felix Bracquemond, whom Poulet-Malassis had asked to produce the design, came up with what Baudelaire furiously termed a 'horror', in which 'the skeleton is walking along and leans on a fan of boughs that branch off his ribs instead of from his arms' (*c*, II, p. 83), and the plan was eventually abandoned.

Baudelaire's rage and dejection can still be felt in a letter he wrote to his mother the day after deriding Bracquemond's drawing, where he depicts himself set about with rapacious creditors, and horrified at the thought that he would die 'without having done anything with [his] life'. For several months, he confesses, 'I have been ill, of an illness from which there is no recovery: cowardice and weakness. Physically this is made worse by my difficulty in sleeping and my bouts of anguish. Sometimes fear, sometimes anger' (*c*, II, p. 84). Yet on the first day of 1861, having just moved once more into new lodgings, he wrote to his mother that despite his continuing unhappiness, he could draw a certain satisfaction from the new edition of his poems:

> *Les Fleurs du mal* is finished. We are in the process of completing the cover and the portrait. There are 35 new poems and each of the old poems has been profoundly revised. For the first time in my life, I am almost content. The book is *almost good*, and it will remain as a witness of my disgust, and my hatred of everything. (*c*, II, pp. 113–4)

Profoundly revised? As is revealed by the diplomatic edition, which reproduces all the poems in all their known versions, Baudelaire rarely reworked his poems extensively once they had been published, preferring to wait until he was satisfied with them before submitting them to the public gaze. Where the proofs of Balzac's novels are covered with a spider's web of his handwritten changes and voluminous additions, and Banville introduced extensive modifications from early publications to later ones, Baudelaire has left us with relatively few variants and, perhaps because of his

Félix Bracquemond, engraving for *Les Fleurs du mal*, 1859.

constant moves within Paris, few of his manuscripts have survived to indicate how much he worked on them. Perhaps, too, he was painting a self-portrait when he slipped the following interpolation into De Quincey's *Confessions*:

> One day a man of genius, melancholy, misanthropic and wanting to avenge himself for his century's injustice, threw all his work, still in manuscript, into the fire. And when reproached for this horrible holocaust made to hatred, which was moreover the sacrifice of all his own hopes, he answered: 'What does it matter? What matters is that they were *created*; they were created and therefore they *are*'. (*MOP*, p. 242)

The palimpsest of memory, he concludes, is indestructible whatever happens to physical remains.

What did change from the 1857 version, however, was the order of the poems. In this new edition we find a far stronger and more complex architecture underpinning the work as a whole. In an often-quoted letter to the older poet Alfred de Vigny, written in mid-December 1861, Baudelaire claimed that the only praise he wanted for his book was that readers 'recognize it is not just an album but has a beginning and an end. All the new poems were written to fit in with the special frame that [he] had chosen' (c, II, p. 196). The greatest alteration concerns the addition of an entire new section: the eighteen poems grouped together as *Parisian Pictures*, which allow Baudelaire to shift poetry's attention away from nature and history, and on to the urban and contemporary. He had moreover expanded the first cycle of love poems, those usually associated with Jeanne Duval, as well as the group inspired by Marie Daubrun, and he had intensified the final section of *Spleen et Idéal* with poems of a particular darkness, such as 'Obsession', 'Alchemy of Suffering', 'Congenial Horror', 'The Clock' and, among his most despairing, 'Longing for Oblivion' with its unforgettably melancholy line: 'Delicious Spring has lost its scent!' (oc, I, p. 76). Three new poems gave both weight and depth to the section called 'Death' as well as bringing the collection as a whole to a bleaker conclusion than in the first edition. 'Day's End' expresses a longing for annihilation; 'The Curious Man's Dream' denies all hope in an afterlife offering anything better than, or even different from, what we have already known, and 'The Voyage' closes with at best the expectation that plunging into the void might bring the discovery of something new.

The volume came out in the first week of February 1861. Few critics in the Parisian press bothered to review it, although the following year the 24-year-old English poet Algernon Swinburne would devote an enthusiastic article to the new edition in *The Spectator*. While the French press might have chosen to ignore Baudelaire's poetry, Asselineau, in the memoirs he devoted to his friend, insists that among young writers he had acquired a considerable reputation, enough to force even the reluctant Sainte-Beuve to recognize in him a master who might rank with Gautier, Banville and Leconte de Lisle.

Hard on the heels of the new edition, however, came the collapse of the precarious shuttle system, in which a group of friends all signed IOUs on behalf of each other. This threatened to plunge both Baudelaire and Poulet-Malassis into bankruptcy. Poulet-Malassis' extraordinary productivity (an 1861 catalogue of his publications reveals the impressive size and high quality of his stable of writers) could not save him from the frequent fines he incurred for publishing works of which the government did not approve, and this, together with a prison sentence for debt, forced him to abandon his Paris shop and retreat to the comparative safety of Belgium. In January 1863, partly to protect himself in this precarious financial position, Baudelaire sold to the publisher Hetzel the rights for the publication of several works, including *Les Fleurs du mal*, although the latter volume had already been sold to Poulet-Malassis. But Baudelaire was never to make much from his writing: Claude Pichois has estimated that by the time he died Baudelaire had been paid less than 10,000 francs for his entire published work, including his translations – less than a third of what he had inherited on coming of age.

Small wonder that a few months after the collapse of the shuttle system of IOUs, Baudelaire wrote his mother a profoundly moving confessional letter. In March, he tells her, he was in 'one of those crises where one sees the terrible truth' (*c*, II, p. 150). In despair about his health, filled with the horror of life, constantly on the brink of suicide, he was nevertheless confident enough in his literary reputation to assert that everything he wrote would be published, even though it would earn him little money. The syphilis he had contracted while still 'very young' had returned and, even worse, had taken a new form, bringing with it 'an extraordinary weariness in all the joints' (*c*, II, p. 152). Feeling old,

he asks: 'Is rejuvenation possible? That's the whole question'
(*c*, II, p. 154). It is a question that frequently recurs in his poems,
too. Pleading with her to allow him to have access to 10,000 francs
from the sum Ancelle controlled, he asserts that this would allow
him to cover his most pressing debts and to live quietly in Honfleur
for a year. After all, he argues persuasively enough, 'I've produced
eight volumes under atrocious circumstances, and can earn my
own living, but I am being assassinated by debt.' We don't have
Mme Aupick's letters to her son, but she either refused or was
unable to help him with this request, which she may in any case
merely have seen as yet another in the painfully long list of his
attempts to regain control of the funds he had shown himself so
woefully incapable of managing.

He continued to publish new poems, including the defiant
'Rebel', the beautiful 'Meditation' and the bleak 'The Lid', all of
which would appear in the posthumous edition of 1868. They cast a
grim light on his state of mind. 'The Rebel' depicts a furious angel
violently whipping a rebel who refuses to accept the Christian law
that one must love 'without grimacing' the poor, the evil, the twisted
and the dull-witted: Baudelaire's dissenter, described by the poem's
end as 'damned', grittily persists in replying: 'I will not' (*oc*, I, pp.
139–40). 'Meditation' is a quietly beautiful sonnet that invites the
poet's personified grief to turn away from the vile multitude of
mortals and look back at past years, until the moment when gentle
Night can be heard walking towards them. In its own way it is also
a meditation on the coming of death. 'The Lid' takes up a theme
already sketched out in the last of the 'Spleen' poems, that of the
sky crushing us from above:

Wherever he goes, on the sea or the dry land,
Under tropical skies or suns bleached of colour
Servant of Jesus or Cythera's courtesan,
Living in opulence or begging in squalor,

City man, countryman, homebound or drifter,
Whether his mind's marked by vigour or languor,
Man sees all around him the mysterious horror
And never looks up without eyes all aquiver.

Above are the Heavens! the stifling cell's roof,
A ceiling lit up for an *opera bouffe*,
Where every ham actor treads boards wet with gore;

The mad hermit's hope, the libertine's terror,
The Heavens! black lid of the great cooking pan
Where simmers the vast, imperceptible family of Man.
(*OC*, I, p. 141)

In parallel with his verse poetry, moreover, Baudelaire had been working for some time on a new kind of poetry, one inspired above all, or so he claims, by the work of Aloysius Bertrand, whose *Gaspard de la Nuit* transposes the familiar verse form of the ballad into prose poetry to create gothic fantasies. Baudelaire had been testing out the possibilities of this new form since the mid-1850s. While prose poetry was not new to France, it is Baudelaire who has given the genre its most distinctive form and flavour, liberating it from its old ties to the forms of verse poetry. In a letter to Hetzel of 20 March 1863 he insisted that he attributed 'great importance' to this collection of prose poems, which, after trying out a series of titles – *Light and Smoke*, *The Solitary Walker*, *The Parisian Prowler* – he now called *Paris Spleen*. These short prose poems he saw as offering a fitting counterpart to *Les Fleurs du mal*, displaying modern life, and primarily contemporary city life, in that 'dangerously' free form, as he called it in his 'Salon of 1859'. It was a genre, he contended, that was intimately associated with large, modern cities, with their countless interconnections, of streets, people and memories. Writing to the novelist, poet and art critic Arsène

Houssaye, in a letter usually included as a preface to the volume, Baudelaire touches on the central attraction of this form for him: 'Who among us has not, in our days of ambition, dreamt of the miracle of a poetic prose, musical without rhythm and rhyme, supple and spasmodic enough to adapt itself to the soul's lyrical movements, to reverie's undulations, to the leaps of conscience?' (*oc*, I, pp. 275–6). Without rhythm and rhyme: what he means, of course, is not that he would completely abandon these two powerful elements of poetry but rather that rhyme and rhythm would break away from prosodic rules and therefore be free to express the ideas and suggestions a specific prose poem explored. The opening sentence of 'We all have our Chimeras', for example, offers both a powerful rhythm reminiscent of pounding feet and a series of alliterations and assonances that tie words together in ways analogous to those of rhyme: 'Under a great, grey sky, on a great, gritty plain, without paths, without grass, not a thistle, not a nettle, I met several men who were walking bent over' (*oc*, I, p. 282). This is what Barbara Johnson has justly termed Baudelaire's second revolution, after that of *Les Fleurs du mal*: a poetry whose modernism stems from a deliberate turn away from the lyrical to the suggestively prosaic, away from the beneficial constraints of form towards a freedom that facilitates a reflection of the chaotic rhythms that characterize the modern city. Not, as some have believed, a minor form or a sign of declining poetical powers, the prose poems are now widely regarded as offering exactly what Baudelaire had claimed for them, a pendant or counterpart to *Les Fleurs du mal*, writing that is both thematically and stylistically as experimental and powerful as the verse poems, and central to the birth of Modernism.

The wind of modernity and the image of the modern artist had, of course, been vital elements of his thinking since the stirring conclusion of the 'Salon of 1845' had placed such emphasis on the heroism of modern life. But the network of ideas associated with them had taken on a particular intensity and clarity with his essay 'The Painter of Modern Life', which he seems to have begun work on in 1859 but which did not appear until the end of 1863. It was published in *Le Figaro*, where it was justly heralded as a work of profound criticism, well researched, and highly original. Ironically, the writer whose initials sign this claim is none other than Gustave Bourdin, the very journalist whose antagonistic 1857 article had alerted the government's attention to *Les Fleurs du mal*. Baudelaire himself, in sending his mother the first part of *Figaro's* publication of his essay, indicated to her that he considered it an important piece of work, but that he was not particularly pleased with Bourdin's preface (*c*, ii, p. 333).

The artist whom Baudelaire selected as his exemplary 'painter of modern life' is ostensibly the relatively minor painter Constantin Guys, whose rapidly executed watercolours offered, in their array of subjects and in the sense they give of an instantaneous transcription of contemporary urban existence, an ideal figure on which Baudelaire could build his idealized portrait. While critics still sometimes accuse Baudelaire of neglecting a truly great painter of

Constantin Guys, *Walk in the Woods*, undated watercolour.

modern life whom he counted among his friends, Edouard Manet, in favour of a far less gifted artist, such criticisms ignore not only the fact that Manet, born in 1832, was at the outset of his career at this point and that Baudelaire had only recently met him, but also and more important still that what Baudelaire sought for the purposes of the essay was, precisely, not the kind of strongly individual personality we find in Manet, but something akin to an artist's lay-figure, on whom he could hang the attributes of an idealized artist. Manet's craggy individualism was already too strong to allow any such thing.

Indeed, the opening paragraphs of 'The Painter of Modern Life' directly address this issue of minor figures and their role in art: 'just because one greatly loves general beauty, which is expressed by the classical poets and artists, that's no reason to neglect specific beauty, the beauty of the occasion' (*oc*, II, p. 683). His interest in certain minor poets (Pétrus Borel, Pierre Dupont and Gustave Le Vavasseur among others) as well as his passion for popular theatre reinforces his commitment to this argument. Beauty, as he argues here, and as he reveals in his prose poems, is relative and historical, not absolute, and while it gives a unified impression, it consists of two main elements: one that is eternal and unchanging, while the other draws on aspects of the time at which it was created, aspects such as fashion, customs or passions. The painter who can capture such fleeting facets, Baudelaire argues revealingly, will therefore be someone whose genius is complex, bringing together characteristics most often associated with the writer, an observer, a philosopher, a *flâneur*. Someone, he implies, very much like himself: 'Sometimes he is a poet. More often he is closer to the novelist and the moralist. He is the painter of the occasion and of all the suggestions of the eternal that lie within the occasion' (*oc*, II, p. 687). Above all, like Poe's character in 'The Man of the Crowds', he hurls himself into the urban masses in search of the unknown, driven by a fatal and irresistible curiosity. Several of Baudelaire's prose poems also illustrate his love of the anonymous crowd, inevitably paired in that complex character with the imperative need for solitude. 'The poet enjoys that incomparable privilege of being able at will to be himself and others. Like those wandering souls in search of a body, he steps, when he wishes to, into everyone's personality' (*oc*, I, p. 291). Bathing in the multitude allowed both the poet and the artist to reveal modern life in all its intensity. Like De Quincey's opium eater, who also found it exhilarating to wander anonymously through the crowds, the painter has much in common with the child, with the child's love of the new, with the child's constant intoxication. Genius, Baudelaire insists, is the intensity of childhood rediscovered at will, but possessed, not of childhood's fragility, but instead of the 'virile organs and analytic mind' necessary to give expression to experience (*oc*, I, p. 690).

Experience in this case is above all that of modernity, which Baudelaire qualifies as the transitive, the fugitive and the contingent (*oc*, II, 695). In order to capture that fleeting impression, the artist resorts not to the polished depictions admired by the academy, but to an abbreviated, shorthand representation that demands an act of imaginative and interpretative memory on the part of the viewer, as in Guys's pen, ink and watercolour depiction of a young woman glimpsed passing by. In the same way, one might argue, the prose poems set out abbreviated visions of the fleeting beauty or charm of contemporary life. An essential part of that charm lies in its unpredictability, hence the need for a form that, unlike the verse poem and particularly unlike the sonnet, however experimental, defies the reader's predictions. For all the poignant beauty of Baudelaire's poem 'To a Passer-by', for example, and despite the relative flexibility of its alexandrines, it cannot equal prose poetry in recreating the abrupt changes of tempo, the collision of multiple rhythms, the noise and movement that the crowded boulevard offers the *flâneur*. There is little doubt that in *Paris Spleen* Baudelaire sought to be like Guys in his rapid sketches: 'always bizarre, violent, excessive, but consistently poetic, he succeeded in concentrating

Constantin Guys, *Young Woman Raising her Skirts as she Walks*, undated, pen and ink with watercolour.

in his sketches the bitter or heady savour of the wine of Life' (*oc*, ii, p. 724).

Delacroix's death in August 1863 enabled Baudelaire to pay tribute to another and very different response to that wine, that of the painter he had most admired since the earliest days of his art criticism, and whom he quoted so often both in his articles and in everyday conversation that his friends began to mock him whenever he said: 'Delacroix was telling me just the other day . . .'. Baudelaire's obituary article for Delacroix sought above all to isolate and define that 'characteristic quality of Delacroix's genius', a quality that had aroused Baudelaire's intense admiration for the 'magic art' with which the painter could 'translate the *word* by painted images more powerful and more nearly exact than any other creator of the same profession' (*oc*, ii, p. 743). While this last essay devoted to the great Romantic painter suggests a certain reticence, a diminution in the unbounded admiration of his youth, and while it does include many passages published elsewhere, it also acts as a further commentary on Baudelaire's image of the modern artist, to an extent where Delacroix, like Guys, at times seems to fade behind a more dominant and generalized picture.

Delacroix's ability to suggest the depths of the soul through contour and colour alone depended in large measure, according to Baudelaire, on a combination of skills: a consummate painter, he also possessed the 'rigour of a discerning writer, and the eloquence of a passionate musician' (*oc*, ii, p. 744). After all, as Baudelaire argues, this was an age in which the various arts aspired not to supplant each other, but rather to lend each other new strength. Such a judgement of course sheds its own light on the poet's sense of his role and of his art. Not only such verse poems as 'The Beacons' and 'The Mask' but also several of his prose poems reflect that determination to draw on the resources of the various arts. Take for example the somewhat extravagant prose poem 'The Desire to Paint' which appeared in the *Revue nationale et étrangère* a few months after Delacroix's death. It was probably inspired by the woman who would be Baudelaire's last mistress, a young actress called Berthe (*oc*, i, p. 1140).

> Unhappy the man but happy the artist lacerated by lust! I burn to paint the woman who appeared so rarely before me and who fled so fast, like something beautiful the traveller regrets to see carried away behind him into the night. How long it is already since she disappeared! She is beautiful, more than beautiful; she is surprising. In her, black abounds and everything she inspires is deep and nocturnal. Her eyes are two caves where mystery sparkles vaguely and her gaze illuminates like a lightning bolt: an explosion in the darkness. (*oc*, i, p. 340)

Not only does Baudelaire revel in the painterly aspects of his task here, but he also clearly delights in the suppleness of a poetic prose that leaves room for both the expanded evocation and the pithy summary, the deliberately pretentious and hyperbolic together with the understated, the suggestive. Delacroix, he would argue in his obituary, 'is the most *suggestive* of all the painters, the one whose works, even selected among those that are secondary and inferior, make one think the most, and recall to the memory the greatest number of poetic sentiments and thoughts already known but that one had believed sunk for ever in the night of the past' (*oc*, ii, p. 745). It is this that makes his canvases – which here at least are reminiscent of Guys' – an aid to memory and makes them particularly expressive of the 'grandeur and inborn passion of the universal individual'. Also like Guys, Delacroix had a passion for notes and sketches, once telling 'a young man of my acquaintance', says Baudelaire, meaning himself: 'If you are not gifted enough to make a sketch of a man throwing himself out of a window in the time it takes him to fall from the fourth floor to the ground, you will never produce a large painting' (*oc*, ii, pp. 763–4). Hyperbole, as Baudelaire admits, but an indication of his determination not to let escape any shred of an action or idea's intensity. It is worth noting the parallel between this demand Delacroix is supposed to have made on the artist and Gautier's assertion, quoted in Baudelaire's first essay on Delacroix, that all writers should have the skills to express any idea, however subtle and unexpected it might be (*oc*, ii, p. 118).

Like Guys, too, Baudelaire depicts Delacroix as 'insatiably curious, a mind open to all notions and all impressions', passionately in love with passion but 'coldly determined to seek out the means of expressing passion in the most visible way possible' (*oc*, ii, p. 740). One sees here the influence of Diderot's paradox of the actor: it is only the actor in complete and cold control of his emotions who can represent a character overwhelmed by emotions. This is the twin mark of the genius for Baudelaire, this combination of great passion yoked to a formidable and lucidly observant will power, and it is perhaps above all what he longed for in himself. Indeed, yet again, this article is perhaps most revealing for what it tells the reader about Baudelaire: Delacroix, he insists, shares this trait with the novelist and politician Prosper Mérimée, in that each throws a 'cloak of ice' over a 'delicate sensitivity and an ardent passion for the good and the beautiful' (*oc*, II, p. 758). Maybe so, but more than either Delacroix or Mérimée that description fits the writer himself, just as the later reference to the painter's propensity for brief maxims concerning how best to lead his life cannot fail to recall Baudelaire's own notebooks with their injunctions to work, their quotations from Emerson – 'The one prudence in life is concentration; the one evil is dissipation' (*oc*, I, p. 674) – and their poignant questions: 'Has my self-centred phase ended?' (*oc*, I, p. 671).

In September 1863 Poulet-Malassis left Paris for Brussels, hoping to restore his lost fortunes in Belgium's less heavily censored book trade. Several poems Baudelaire publishes around this time suggest his own longing to break free from the existence he had forged for himself, together with his profound scepticism, based on weary experience, about the possibility of any such escape. The prose poem 'Already', published in December 1863, is characteristically capable of seeing both the temptation and the probable results. It depicts a group of travellers, whose long sea voyage has brought them far enough south for them to be able to 'decipher the celestial alphabet of the antipodes' and who long for the physical comforts of dry land. We can recognize among them some of the figures who populate 'The Voyage', those who were delighted to flee an infamous country, those who sought to escape the horror of their homes, and those who were breaking free from a tyrannical woman. In the prose poem we find them already possessed of the 'bitter knowledge' (*oc*, I, p. 133) that comes from travel, dreaming of the homes they had been so eager to leave and longing for their unfaithful and grumpy wives. But, as we know, the true voyagers are those who leave for the sake of leaving, and the narrator of the prose poem finds himself unimaginably sad as land approaches and he is forced to bid farewell to the sea which is 'so monstrously seductive and so infinitely varied' and seems to contain and represent through its 'games, movement, rages and smiles, the moods, the suffering and the ecstasies of all the souls that have lived, who live now, and who will live in the future' (*oc*, I, p. 338). Dreaming of moving to a different country while staying comfortably at home, like inventing stories about other people rather than actually meeting them ('The Windows'), or imagining what it would be like to make love in a variety of different places ('The Projects'), all seemed more important than external reality, although in a different mood Baudelaire's soul, offered a menu of tempting places to visit, could scream at him: 'Anywhere! Anywhere! Just as long as it's outside this world!' (*oc*, I, p. 357).

Since going beyond the world was not possible, on 24 April 1864 Baudelaire left Paris for Brussels. His hope was to earn money by giving a series of lectures and readings, and to secure publishing contracts with the Belgian firm of Lacroix and Verboeckhoven, the publishing house used by Victor Hugo, then still in exile from Napoleon III's régime. Suitably enough for the intellectual dandy that he was, he stayed at the Hotel du Grand Miroir, named for its first owner, Engelbert de Speculo. But as so often, Baudelaire's speculations were ill-founded. His lectures on Delacroix, Gautier and the artificial paradises, as well as his readings of his own poetry, not only earned him considerably less than he had imagined, but failed to attract the publishers Lacroix and Verboeckhoven, although he had sent them personal invitations. Once again Baudelaire was consumed with rage, but this time his fury proved destructive rather than creative.

Refusing to leave Brussels, however much he detested it and with it Belgium and its inhabitants as a whole, he spent much of the rest of that year and the following one gathering a series of biting epigrams attacking what he presented as the materialism, stupidity and gluttony of the entire nation. Satire, as Juvenal's brilliant poems and Hugo's cumulatively tedious work, *Les Châtiments*, each differently demonstrate, has to be leavened by wit, however excoriating, and by the awareness that the self is also implicated in the attacks made against individuals or against humanity at large. Baudelaire's prose poem 'Portraits of Mistresses', which he seems to have written while in Belgium, can be read as a rather more urbane version of Juvenal's sixth satire, with its attacks on women and its suggestion that a perfect wife, that *rara avis*, would prove not just tedious but infuriating for her ability to show up the faults of her husband. In the prose poem, the lover of this perfect woman confesses to three companions that he murdered her – 'What else could I have done with her, *given that she was perfect*?' – forcing his less 'rigorous' companions, like Baudelaire's hypocrite readers, to pretend not to have understood the confession. The poem ends with all of them ordering more bottles, 'to kill Time, which clings so stubbornly to life, and to accelerate Life, that flows so slowly' (*OC*, I, p. 349). The poet doesn't separate himself from his characters, and the men are shown in just as jaundiced a light as the women they denounce. But Baudelaire's collection of epigrams for *Pauvre Belgique!* has, at least in the note form in which he left it, little of that leavening and little, too, of that brilliance of language that also marks Juvenal's satires.

Homesickness, despite his rage against Paris, pervades the notes for *Pauvre Belgique!* Brussels is noisier than Paris, he comments, grumbling that the roads are poorly laid, the people clumsy, the animals noisy, where Paris, although 'infinitely greater and busier, produces merely a vast and vague humming, a velvety humming, so to speak' (*OC*, II, p. 825). If adorable spring had lost its perfume, the excitement of plunging into the crowd had also turned sour: 'In a crowd, the Belgian shoves the person in front of him as hard as he can with both fists. The only possible response is to turn around abruptly, giving him, as if by mistake, a vigorous jab in the stomach with your elbow' (*oc*, II, p. 832). Good conversation, tasty food, feminine beauty: all this might exist in Brussels, he confesses, but behind closed doors, in the intimacy of the home, from which he was so implacably excluded.

Back in France, ironically, Baudelaire was beginning to enter into that regard and respect that part of him so craved, even if at another level he both feared and despised it. Poulet-Malassis made use of the freedom of the press in Belgium to publish, as part of a volume entitled *Parnasse satirique du dix-neuvième siècle*, the poems that had been excised from the first edition of *Les Fleurs du mal*. Many of Baudelaire's prose poems and later verse poems, as well as his translations of Poe, were appearing in the press. In February 1865 the young poet Stéphane Mallarmé published in *L'Artiste* a 'literary symphony' the second part of which was devoted to Baudelaire and which began: 'In winter, when my torpor leaves me, I plunge with delight into the beloved pages of *Les Fleurs du mal*. Scarcely have I opened my Baudelaire than I am drawn into a surprising landscape that comes to life under my gaze with the intensity of those created by profound opium'.[6] The piece is not only a meditation on Baudelaire's themes but also a brilliant pastiche of his style, reminiscent in this technique of Baudelaire's own finest literary criticism. And at the end of 1865 *L'Art* published three fervent articles on him, written by the young Paul Verlaine, he who, as an adolescent, had first bought a copy of Baudelaire's poems under the impression that the book, rapidly glanced at, was called *Les Fleurs de Mai* (*The Flowers of May*).

Ill, devoured with anger, and too proud to return to Paris before he had somehow recovered from his debts, Baudelaire found some consolation in the friendship of Poulet-Malassis, to whom he sent a copy of one of the most moving photographs ever taken of him; that taken by Charles Neyt. The poet has written on it: 'To my friend Auguste Poulet-Malassis, sole being whose smile lightened my sorrow in Belgium'. The hair has turned white, the lines between mouth and nose are more deeply scored, the thin-lipped mouth has

Charles Neyt, *Baudelaire*, 1864–5, photograph autographed by Baudelaire to Auguste Poulet-Malassis.

a bitter twist to it, but the clothes still suggest the intellectual dandy and the eyes continue to gaze piercingly at the lens.

There was some form of consolation, too, in the pleasure he took in the beautiful, airy Jesuit churches of Belgium, full of light, and his sole source of architectural enjoyment (*oc*, II, p. 944). He admired the magnificent stained glass windows of the high Gothic church of Saint Gudula: 'beautiful intense colours, like those a profound soul projects over the objects of life' (*oc*, II, p. 942). He travelled to the Belgian town of Namur, situated at the confluence of the Sambre and the Meuse and the site of numerous churches.

His visit was characteristically marked by his awareness of the town's association with the seventeenth-century French writer Nicolas Boileau, who devoted one of his satires to the siege of Namur, and of the Flemish painter Adam Frans Van der Meulen, as well as by his fascination with the Jesuit style, which he considered as possessing a particular majesty, inundated with light as these churches are through their great windows (*oc*, II, p. 952). He tells himself that once and for all he must 'characterize the beauty of this style (late Gothic)' (*oc*, II, p. 951) and notes in particular the 'sinister and gallant marvel' of the Church of Saint-Loup, with its interior like a catafalque embroidered with black, pink and silver. It was in the desire to prepare a 'technical description (insofar as I can)' (*oc*, II, p. 952) of Saint-Loup that he returned to the town in March 1866. While visiting the church in the company of Poulet-Malassis and the artist Félicien Rops Baudelaire collapsed, victim of a stroke. His last letter, written at his dictation and dated Friday, 30 March, was to his mother. He begged her to write to him but also to tell Ancelle not to bother coming, explaining that he could not move, was still in debt, and still had six towns to visit, since he did not wish 'to lose the fruit of much work' (*c*, II, p. 632). It was the day on which he would become paralysed on his right side, the day on which he seems to have lost that wonderful control of language that had been his most remarkable gift. On 2 July he was taken back to Paris by his mother and his painter friend Arthur Stevens. He died just over a year later, on 31 August 1867.

'Where a genius is concerned, the public is a watch running slow' (*oc*, II, p. 751), Baudelaire had claimed of Delacroix. Ironically, Michel Lévy would begin publishing his complete works in 1868, the first biographies began to appear soon after, but it was not until 31 May 1949 that the sentence against the excised poems was finally quashed. By 1957, however, the centenary of the first publication of *Les Fleurs du mal*, the French national library's exhibition of his life and work drew huge crowds. Now, a century and a

Félix Nadar, *Charles Baudelaire, c.* 1855.

half after that publication, Baudelaire is recognized as one of the
great poets of western civilisation, not only for *Les Fleurs du mal*,
which introduced new themes and a new vocabulary as well as
rendering the standard verse forms incomparably supple, but also
for his *Paris Spleen*, where his image of prose poetry served to
define the genre and the evocation of the complexity of city life
laid the foundations for Modernism.

It is best to take our leave of him with Nadar's photograph, from around 1855: leaning back in a handsome armchair, the high dome of his forehead still unlined, his left hand delicately placed against his cheek, he appears lost in a blend of creative reverie and a sceptical assessment of the contemporary world.

References

1 Childhood and Youth

1 Claude Pichois and Jean Ziegler, *Baudelaire* (Paris, 1987), p. 112.
2 Pichois and Ziegler, *Baudelaire*, p. 118.
3 On this see Graham Robb, *La Poésie de Baudelaire et la poésie française 1838–1852* (Paris, 1993).
4 Claude Pichois, *La Jeunesse de Baudelaire* (Nashville, TE, 1991), pp. 19–20.
5 Pichois, *Jeunesse*, p. 50.
6 Ibid.
7 Pichois and Ziegler, *Baudelaire*, p. 626.

2 Revolt

1 Eugène Crépet, *Charles Baudelaire* (Paris, 1928), p. 26.
2 Claude Pichois and Jean Ziegler, *Baudelaire* (Paris, 1987), p. 158.
3 Pichois and Ziegler, *Baudelaire*, p. 162.
4 Claude Pichois, *La Jeunesse de Baudelaire* (Nashville, TE, 1991), p. 92.
5 Champfleury [Jules Husson], *Souvenirs et portraits de jeunesse* (Paris, 1872), p. 135.
6 *Baudelaire et Asselineau*, eds. Jacques Crépet and Claude Pichois (Paris, 1953), pp. 66–8.
7 Pichois, *La Jeunesse de Baudelaire*, pp. 23–4.
8 A. Privat d'Anglemont, *Paris inconnu* (Paris, 1861) pp. 343–4.

9 Pichois, *La Jeunesse de Baudelaire*, p. 23.

10 Pichois, *La Jeunesse de Baudelaire*, p. 52.

11 Quoted in A. Tabarant, *La Vie artistique au temps de Baudelaire* (Paris, 1963), p. 81.

12 *Baudelaire and Asselineau*, pp. 76–7.

3 Second Empire Paris

1 Théodore de Banville, *Œuvres poétiques complètes*, ed. Peter Edwards (Geneva, 1992–2001), vol. III, p. 51.

2 Claude Pichois and Jacques Dupont, *L'Atelier de Baudelaire* (Paris, 2005), p. 3070.

3 Pichois and Dupont, *L'Atelier*, p. 2687.

4 Quoted in Claude Pichois and Jean Ziegler, *Baudelaire* (Paris, 1987), p. 301.

5 Pichois and Dupont, *L'Atelier*, p. 1849.

4 The Results of the Trial

1 Richard D. E. Burton, *Baudelaire in 1859* (Cambridge, 1988), p. 182.

2 Sotheby's catalogue, *100 Livres, Manuscrits, Documents & Objets littéraires de la collection Pierre Leroy, 27 June 2007*, p. 54.

3 Maxime Du Camp, *Les Chants Modernes* (Paris, 1855), p. 5.

4 *Lettres à Baudelaire*, ed. Claude Pichois (Neuchâtel, 1973), p. 382.

5 W. T. Bandy, and Claude Pichois, *Baudelaire devant ses contemporains* (Paris, 1967), pp. 164–5.

5 The Final Years

1 W. T. Bandy and Claude Pichois, *Baudelaire devant ses contemporains* (Paris, 1967), pp. 30–31.

2 Bandy and Pichois, *Baudelaire devant ses contemporains*, p. 31.

3 Philibert Audibrand, *Un Café de journalistes sous Napoléon III* (Paris, 1888) p. 295.

4 Charles Yriarte, *Portraits cosmopolites* (Paris, 1870), p. 124.

5 Yriarte, *Portraits cosmopolites*, p. 120.

6 Stéphane Mallarmé, *Œuvres complètes*, ed. Bertrand Marchal (Paris, 2003), vol. II, p. 282.

Further Reading

Editions

The standard edition of Baudelaire's complete works is the one published by Gallimard in its Pléiade series and edited by the great Baudelaire scholar Claude Pichois (Paris, 1975–6). Equally, the best source for the correspondence is Pichois' edition for the same series (Paris, 1972), supplemented with *Nouvelles Lettres de Baudelaire* (Paris, 2000) and *Lettres à Baudelaire* (Neuchâtel, 1973). For a valuable edition of Baudelaire's translation of De Quincey in parallel with the English original, see *Un Mangeur d'Opium*, edited by Michèle Stäuble (Neuchâtel, 1976). A useful single volume edition of the works with a selection of letters is the *Œuvres complètes*, published by Editions Robert Laffont (Paris, 1980).

Biographies

The most detailed biography is that by Claude Pichois and Jean Ziegler (Paris, 1987) of which Graham Robb has produced a shortened version in English: *Baudelaire* (London, 1987). Numerous other English biographies exist including Enid Starkie, *Baudelaire* (Harmondsworth, 1971); Alex de Jong, *Baudelaire, Prince of Clouds: A Biography* (New York, 1976); R. L. Williams, *The Horror of Life* (Chicago, IL, 1980); F.W.J. Hemmings, *Baudelaire the Damned: A Biography* (New York, 1982) and Joanna Richardson, *Baudelaire* (New York, 1994). Richard D. E. Burton's *Baudelaire in 1859:*

A Study in the Sources of Poetic Creativity (Cambridge, 1988) is a detailed exploration of one year of the poet's life. For reflections of the young Baudelaire in the writing of the time see Claude Pichois, ed., *La Jeunesse de Baudelaire vue par ses amis: lettres à Eugène Crépet. Textes retrouvés par Eric Dayre* (Nashville, TE, 1991).

Translations

For a comparative study of translations of Baudelaire's poetry see my *Baudelaire's World* (Ithaca, NY, 2002). Clive Scott, *Translating Baudelaire* (Exeter, 2000) offers a lively and individualistic view of the whole question. Carol Clark and Robert Sykes have gathered various different translations in *Baudelaire in English* (Harmondsworth, 1997). Recent translations of *Les Fleurs du mal* include Richard Howard, *Les Fleurs du mal* (Boston, 1982); Walter Martin, *The Complete Poems of Baudelaire* (Manchester, 1997); James McGowan, *The Flowers of Evil* (Oxford, 1993); Francis Scarfe, *The Complete Verse of Baudelaire* (London, 1986); and Norman R. Shapiro, *Selected Poems from Les Fleurs du mal* (Chicago, 1998).

The prose poems have been translated by Edward Kaplan, *The Parisian Prowler* (Athens, GA, 1997); Francis Scarfe, *Charles Baudelaire: The Poems in Prose* (London, 1989) and myself, *Baudelaire's The Prose Poems and La Fanfarlo* (Oxford, 1991).

For translations of Baudelaire's so-called journals see Norman Cameron, *Intimate Journals* (New York, 1995) and Christopher Isherwood, *Intimate Journals* (Boston, 1957). Jonathan Mayne has translated the art criticism in two volumes: *Art in Paris 1845–1862* (London, 1965) and *The Painter of Modern Life* (London, 1964). The artificial paradises have been translated most recently by Patricia Roseberry, *Artificial Paradise* (Harrogate, 1999).

The poetry

For a lucid, brief exploration of *Les Fleurs du mal* see Alison Fairlie,
Baudelaire: 'Les Fleurs du mal' (London, 1960). An excellent analysis of his
poetic techniques can be found in Graham Chesters, *Baudelaire and the
Poetics of Craft* (Cambridge, 1988). Fine recent studies of the prose poems
are by Marie Maclean, *Narrative as Performance: The Baudelairean
Experience* (London, 1988); Sonya Stephens, *Baudelaire's Prose Poems: The
Practice and Politics of Irony* (Oxford, 1999); Steve Murphy, *Logiques du
dernier Baudelaire: Lectures du 'Spleen de Paris'* (Paris, 2003) and Maria C.
Scott, *Baudelaire's 'Le Spleen de Paris'* (Aldershot, 2005). For the popularity
of poetry at the time see Graham Robb, *La Poésie de Baudelaire et la poésie
française 1838–1852* (Paris, 1993).

Art criticism

For the background to Baudelaire's art reviews see A. Tabarant, *La Vie
artistique au temps de Baudelaire* (Paris, 1963) and T. J. Clark, *The Absolute
Bourgeois. Artists and Politics in France: 1848–1851* (London, 1973). James
Hiddleston offers a fine general reading of the art criticism in *Baudelaire
and the Art of Memory* (Oxford, 1999) as does Timothy Raser, *A Poetics of
Art Criticism: The Case of Baudelaire* (Chapel Hill, NC, 1989). A very useful
and copiously illustrated edition of the 'Salon of 1846' is that of David
Kelley (Oxford, 1975). On the essays about laughter and caricature see
Michèle Hannoosh, *Baudelaire and Caricature: From the Comic to an Art of
Modernity* (University Park, PA, 1992). Various books reproduce the works
that Baudelaire discusses in his art criticism and mentions in his poetry.
Among the best of these are Yann le Pichon and Claude Pichois, *Le Musée
retrouvé de Charles Baudelaire* (Paris, 1992) and Jean-Paul Avice and Claude
Pichois, *Passion Baudelaire: L'ivresse des images* (Paris, 2003).

The literary criticism

On this see Margaret Gilman, *Baudelaire the Critic* (New York, 1943) and my *Baudelaire's Literary Criticism* (Cambridge, 1981)

Baudelaire and music

The best recent study devoted to Baudelaire and Wagner is that of Margaret Miner, *Resonant Gaps between Baudelaire and Wagner* (Athens, GA, 1993).

Baudelaire and the city

Walter Benjamin's inspired readings of Baudelaire as *flâneur* have been gathered together in *The Writer of Modern Life*, ed. Michael W. Jennings (Cambridge, MA, 2006). See also Ross Chamber's *Loiterature* (Lincoln, NE, 1999). The catalogue for the Bibliothèque historique de la Ville de Paris's exhibition *Baudelaire/Paris* (Paris, 1993) offers a superb collection of illustrations linking the poet and the city.

Acknowledgements

My debt to previous Baudelaire biographers and scholars will be evident. Like all readers of Baudelaire I am immensely grateful to the late Claude Pichois, whose tireless devotion to Baudelaire I have long admired. I am also particularly indebted to the work of the following: Lloyd James Austin, Alison Fairlie and Felix Leakey. Among the many whose readings of Baudelaire have illuminated my own understanding, I would like to offer special thanks to Richard Burton, Ross Chambers, Michèle Hannoosh, Patrick Labarthe, Steve Murphy and Sonya Stephens.

Photo Acknowledgements

The author and publishers wish to express their thanks to the following sources of illustrative material and/or permission to reproduce it (some locations of artworks are also given below):

Photos © Adoc-photos/Art Resource, NY: pp. 80 (ART318125), 117 (ART305194), 149 (ART307713; photo by Bayar and Bertall); photo Arnaudet/Réunion des Musées Nationaux/Art Resource, NY: p. 47 (ART154825); photos Michèle Bellot/Réunion des Musées Nationaux/Art Resource, NY: pp. 43 (ART166740), 110 (ART166742); Bibliothèque Historique de la Ville de Paris: p. 92, 173; Bibliothèque Nationale de France, Paris: pp. 96, 131; photos Bridgeman-Giraudon/Art Resource, NY: pp. 120 (ART28184), 131 (ART69055), 163 (ART26886); Château de Compiègne: p. 47 (Inv. c.60.004); Fondazione Magnani Rocca, Corte di Mamiano, Italy: p. 143; photo C. Jean/Réunion des Musées Nationaux/Art Resource, NY: p. 166 (ART168380); photos Erich Lessing/Art Resource, NY: pp. 31 (ART58540), 49 (ART93175), 71 (ART64352), 73 (ART119772), 129 (4644); courtesy The Lilly Library, Indiana University, Bloomington, Indiana: pp. 11, 81, 142; Mahmoud Khalil Museum, Cairo: p. 71; Mary Evans Picture Library/The Image Works: p. 122 (EMEP0117195), The Metropolitan Museum of Art, New York: p. 119 (Catharine Lorillard Wolfe Collection, Wolfe Fund, 1916, 16.39; photo © The Metropolitan Museum of Art/Art Resource, NY - ART323132); Musée des Arts Décoratifs, Paris: p. 163; Musée Carnavalet, Paris: p. 157; Musée Fabre, Montpellier: p. 73; Musée National du Palais de Versailles: p. 49; Musée d'Orsay, Paris: pp. 31 (RF 2257), 33 (Inv. PHO1968-74), 43 (RF 41644), 109 (top), 121 (PHO1985-224), 175; Musée